*My Joburg
Family*

First publication 2023 by Footprint Press, South Africa

email: david@footprintpress.co.za
website: www.footprintpress.co.za

Copyright © Glenn Babb

Page layout by Anthony Cuerden
Email: ant@flyingant.co.za

Printed by Creda Press

ISBN: 978-0-63980-506-1

All rights reserved. No part of this publication may be reproduced, stored, manipulated in any retrieval system, or transmitted in any mechanical, electronic form or by any other means, without the prior written authority of the publishers, except for short extracts in media reviews. Any person who engages in any unauthorized activity in relation to this publication shall be liable to criminal prosecution and claims for civil and criminal damages.

My Joburg Family

Glenn Babb

" Thethil wath a caterpillar.
Thethil wath MY friend.
The latht time I thaw Thethil,
he was this big."

Foreword

My Joburg Family brought back a flood of memories, a feeling of déjà vu, which would surely be shared by members of this generation when reading the book.

When I think back to my childhood and growing up in Johannesburg in the 60s and 70s, I almost feel guilty as it was the happiest of times.

As a child, there was tennis and all sorts of games outside, Mum horse-riding with us, children climbing trees and chasing the guinea fowl, watching my father and uncle playing polo at the Inanda Club, Elias our driver in the yellow Valiant taking my brother and me to The Ridge School, butter balls at all meals, Mr Pete our butler at Springwaters and his love for Kaiser Chiefs, the afternoon summer lightning storms, the dry winters, and the holidays to Sheffield Beach at Easter and Hermanus for Christmas.

But there was always an edginess about living in Johannesburg, a grittiness to the city, with a feeling that we were somehow special but weren't the centre of the universe even though so many Jo'burgers had pretensions to be so.

And that the future had an element of dread. And that we may not live there forever.

It was the best of times.

Robert Hersov, chairman and CEO of Invest Africa

Contents

My Joburg Family
1

The Old Girl and the Old Man
9

Three Boys
91

Some Reflections on St John's
109

Back to the Family
121

Joys and Sorrows
139

My Joburg Family Tree
158

Back to the Grindstone
161

Mandy
171

Triptych of great-grannie Ora in youth, maturity and dotage

My Joburg Family

Take me back to ol' Joburg
Where the elektriese light always shines
And the trams run down to new Fordsburg
And the mine hooters tell me the time.

The mining camp, the town, the city of the Jameson Raiders imprisoned in the Fort, of the miners' strike, the Vorster Gang in the Kensington hills, of Miss Bagg, dead under the bridge on Atholl Oaklands Rd, of Bubbles Schroeder killed by David Polliack and Hymie Leibman, and of the suicide-murder of Brett Kebble, is Joburg, the city of gold. President Paul Kruger would not allow a direct railway line between Joburg and Pretoria, the capital, so fiercely did he decry the louche goings-on a mere 50 kilometres away; so, we travel to Germiston first before reaching the puritanical heights of the capital city. All the city centre streets have a kink in them at Jeppe Street because, in the wild days, two town planners divided the planning spoils North-South, one calculating in yards, the other in metres.

Along with the haste, the impatience and the bustle, came a destructive trait, which pushed obstacles out of the way, and a natural impulsiveness. Joburg was born the same year as Vancouver, 1886. To celebrate this coetaneous existence, Vancouver sent Johannesburg an Indian totem pole 35 feet high that stood proudly in Joubert Park till it became shabby and the council unceremoniously removed this brotherly gesture of twinship to the rubbish tip. Sentimentality does not characterise such a callow and brusque community, with its sharp elbows. When the mining company, Germiston Deep, could find no takers for the oldest wooden headgear in the world, made of teak, it burnt it. Just as Killarney Studios burnt the reels and reels of historic film in its courtyard on Riviera Road, Killarney, and had the temerity to boast of this Guy Fawkes pyre and show it on its iconic *African Mirror* news shorts.

Buildings of unique value fell under the Philistines' wrecking ball. One of the finest examples of art déco, the 21-storey Eskom Building on the corner of Main and Rissik Streets, was once the tallest building in Africa. It had a fan-shaped conference room with cinema provision for "talkies". It lasted less than fifty years from 1936 to 1983 and ironically, in its entrance hall, etched on black glass, sure of the new engineering might Joburg now displayed, stood the legend: "Dedicated to the ideal of cementing together with common endeavour for achievement, all the peoples of South Africa regardless of race or creed into a brotherhood of mutual trust and goodwill for the welfare of our country and the Glory of Almighty God". Not much of that left.

The other wonder of the movie era, the Colosseum Theatre, built in 1933, a thousand-seater with stars in the ceiling, gargoyles on the boxes, velvet seats and a "ladies' powder room" with a round bench and golden statues in the alcoves was demolished by Liberty Life Insurance. Only by dint of some late-awakening citizens was the other art déco wonder, Anstey's building (1937), saved from the same fate in 1989. Were Joburgers slowly changing their philosophy of knowing the price of everything and the value of nothing?

Harry Oppenheimer, the greatest beneficiary of Joburg's cornucopia, donated a city block for the Ernest Oppenheimer Park which sported the leaping impala fountain, and created an open space in the overbuilt centre. Like the Rissik Street Post Office, the bronze was too tempting for the vandals who cut bits off and it has removed to the front of the Anglo-American Building at 44 Main Street.

Joburgers know they suffer from an image of barbarity and of roughness. To mitigate this, almost unwittingly, they have erected and created some gems, which, like the mine headgear, go unappreciated.

> "Breathes there a man with soul so dead
> Who never to himself hath said:
> 'This is my own, my native land'
> Whose heart hath ne'er within him burned
> As home his footsteps he hath turned
> From wandering on a foreign strand."

Because of the coarseness, the odd gems shine ever brighter. Stand on Eastwold Avenue in Saxonwold, under the mauve canopy of the jacarandas meeting over the road at sunset and watch, in the West, the orange horizon rise up through the arches of the achingly beautiful memorial to the Joburg Boer War dead superimposed with an angel of death and feel the chill of the Highveld darkness as the red suddenly sinks into velvet black.

Stand at the top of Acorn Lane in Observatory and look South over the chrome yellow of the goldmine dumps whose fine dust swirls and stings your cheeks in the sharp south wind. There they squat, the leftovers of the wealth extracted from stone underneath, from below sea level even though Joburg is six thousand feet above that sea.

Stand at the bend of Munro Drive in Houghton and peer north over the sea of jacarandas at the distant Voortrekker Monument from your neatly chipped sandstone vantage point. Below are the sturdy homes of the wealthy, practical and bourgeois. The swimming pools and tennis courts smooth out the plain at your feet.

Those uncultured burghers, Jews, Greeks, Scots, Italians, Portuguese, Germans, this potpourri wanted, in some way, maybe even guiltily, to give a tip, a pourboire to the city that nurtured their move up the bourgeoisie ladder. Hermann Eckstein, the German founder of the Chamber of Mines and the Rand Club had joined up in business with Alfred Beit, and after his death, Beit's company planted, in his memory, three million trees in the area Eckstein called *"Sachsenwald"*, now Saxonwold, and

Forest Town. Joburg then became known as the world's largest man-made forest. Zoo Lake and the Joburg Zoo were part of the bequest that made up the Beit Company parcel – a commission it paid in exchange for the wealth it acquired. Like Cecil John Rhodes, Eckstein was the son of a pastor.

When the Johannesburg Art Museum bought a Picasso Harlequin in pastel and crayon at R55,000, the longest serving councillor on the Joburg Council, Obie Oberholzer, proposed and succeeded in reducing the city's subsidy to the museum to zero and commissioning, at almost a million rands, a bronze statue of George Harrison, the purported discoverer of gold, to stand at the east entry to Johannesburg. Strauss & Co assesses the Picasso at several million now and the Harrison statue at the price of the bronze.

As the mining camp transmogrified into a sturdy city, the city became adorned with robust buildings, ever aware that they, too, could be flattened without scruple or regret. The whole of Houghton Ridge, where the mining magnates had built their Edwardian piles, made way for the *blokhaus* Johannesburg General Hospital. There was a new sheriff in town when the Nats took over in 1948. Nat architects constructed squat churches that they thought presented a modernising influence through the inevitable bare, bleak, hard, yellowish bricks and tall steeples, even in places where the Dutch Reformed congregations were small, like Norwood. It is as if they were saying: "That'll show the *rooinekke*."

The granite solidity of the new rich burghers resisted the destruction: the burghers had ambition to becoming stolid citizens, less transient, surer of themselves and erecting the granite Johannesburg Library, haughty with three arches looking over their noses at the library gardens, the sherry queens and down-and-outs, the City Hall, sandstone, opened by the Duke of Connaught in 1910, and its attendant Selborne Hall and, as is only appropriate, the Headquarters of Anglo-American Corporation at 44 Main St. which Anglo American abandoned to move to Rosebank in 2021 thereby eviscerating, at last, central Joburg of the last gold-mining headquarters.

You need to be tough to live on the Witwatersrand, the white-water ridge, where the gold seams lie underground – one seam directly below Anglo American's headquarters. The winters are chill. Thin layers of ice stretch over the fishponds. The land is barren. The grass whitens. There are no rivers and that's why the tribes dispersed by Mzilikazi did not settle there. Beware the dryness of the air. The shock of static when you touch your car door can make you jump backwards. For Joburg, water and warmth could only be found elsewhere. Water came from the Braamfontein, Doornfontein and Turffontein springs and the Klip River, not enough for a town of more than 100,000 by 1906. Barney Barnato monopolised the supply. Coal heated every home, made the energy, powered the industries. Everywhere there were coal storages and transport companies brought the lumps to your door. "Mac won't Phail you", Wolperts. It all came from the coalfields in the Eastern Transvaal, to which the mining companies expanded their corporate diversification in Witbank and Middelburg. Smoke hovered over the city, especially over Alexandra township where every worker had an open coal stove. A brown haze clings to the air.

The seasons in Joburg consist of winter and summer. By the time the cosmos flowers have withered, the storms start. Civil service rain. At five, almost every evening, the black clouds gather in the South. The sky looms above and splits with sheet lightning and cloud-to-earth lightning strikes corrugated iron roofs directly. Thunder rolls and vibrates the air like an earthquake. Every house has a lightning rod. Heavy drops explode the dry grass and dust into the air, the gutters overflow and rivulets course down every hill. Don't walk in the *sloots*, you will be washed away. The hail can pepper the tin roofs and dent your car. The winter is over. The jacaranda blossoms luxuriate in every street. The golf courses have greens again and golfers can now find the white ball. Summer ends with the last rains at the start of the Rand Easter Show.

After the storm, the scent, the odour, the fragrance of the damp earth imbues the air. It is more delicious than baking bread. The steam raises red clay aromas to your nostrils. The snails begin to creep. White ants, termites, in their swarms emerge from their heaps, dropping their diaphanous wings. To perfect the moment, the coucal, the *vleiloerie*, begins its waterfall decrescendo.

Each house has a corrugated iron tank to take off the rain from the gutters, some rusted at the seams. The water should last to next winter, but the mosquitoes breed there. Luckily, the Highveld is too cold for the *anopheles* mosquito and its malaria.

Joburgers liked their entertainment of the music hall variety. The horses prevailed. Two racetracks brought in the punters who emulated the sophistication of the Oppenheimers who were (are) owners and breeders of racehorses, Germiston and Turffontein. Bookmakers were all over Joburg, newspapers bear front-page reports on the races which have prizes calculated in guineas. But, for the others, there is a dog-racing track near Park Station closed down by the Nats because the Dutch Reformed Church disapproved of gambling – but the horses are saved because too many Afrikaners are breeders. The speedway, cinder track and dirt track ovals filled up on Friday evenings, the crowd hoping that a crash would enliven an otherwise dull day. Buddy Fuller ruled the roost on two-wheeled Norton 350cc and 500cc bikes but also at stock car races where crashes were guaranteed and encouraged.

In emulation of the English, the Joburg entertainment complex was Wembley – Wembley ice- rink, Wembley soccer stadium, Wembley racetrack. The northern suburb social round copied the English, with tea, tennis and bridge. Of their politics, it was said that Joburgers spoke Progressive, voted UP and thanked God for the Nats. Each year they attended the pantomime at His Majesty's Theatre, they went to Boswell's Circus which featured the undying Tickey the Clown, they celebrated Guy Fawkes and threw money to the students at the annual University Rag. Now no longer so dependent on mining, Joburgers flocked to the Rand Easter Show to get samples of the new home-grown products of industry and to watch the show-jumping.

Joburg had only existed for 57 years when I was born into it at the

Florence Nightingale and the grinding of the new ship's timbers had comfortably become a fixed orderliness of society not prone to the turmoil of unexpected upheavals. My father had lived there almost all his life and gone to St John's College in Joburg and my mother had moved there on marriage to him. Their antecedents, also my mother's, had reached Joburg as young people. Joburg had its own rhythm, its own ambitions, its own prejudices by the time I joined its carousel. The Babbs were Joburgers as few could be.

Anstey's Building,
Joubert Street, Joburg

Mom debutante

Dad and Hugh on Adderley St

The Old Girl and the Old Man

Growing into teenagehood, Joburgers did not speak to others of "Mum and Dad". Parents were called "the old girl and the old man" and sometimes even "the old queen", except when addressing them directly. My mother preferred the term "mom". She had been overawed by the USA when she visited together with my father on a business trip in 1947. The American idolatry must have had its effect beforehand, though, because all her sons got American names – Wayne, Glenn and Judson. She was a bit remorseful when she later learnt that Judson meant son of a Jew, towards whom she had an ambivalent attitude. One of my father's business principals bore the name Judson Puffer which had inspired my mother. The house-help always called him Jackson or Jickson. My own name can only have come from Glenn Ford and Glenn Miller, whereas Wayne means waggoner in England but its popularity as a forename spiked in the US in the 30s.

The names of our forebears cascaded out of the Victorian and Edwardian psalter: Charles Homer, Horace Edwin, Cecil Victor, Nina Italia, Ora, Ora Constance, Maude.

Like everyone I know, I regret not having asked my parents the questions I want answered now about relatives, times of events, relationships and causes. I want to know from what clay we are formed. They are dead, so any new information comes from third parties, from memories or from scraps in letters and official reports. My account of the old girl and the old man is filtered by time and by allusions.

What characterised our family life was the permanence of things. We lived our whole childhood in the same house. The neighbours were almost all the same throughout. The boys went to the same school from the age of five. My parents never divorced. The circle of their friends only changed glacially. As a polite title, the close friends got the title "uncle" or "auntie", a Cape affectation my mother brought with her from Cape Town. Uncle Bob, Auntie Sheila, Uncle Jacko, Auntie Mickey, Auntie Winnie. The furniture stayed the same. When the cats' claws had shredded the material on the corners of the couches (never sofas, that was non-U) in the sitting room (never lounge, that was non-U), the old girl had them re-upholstered then new patterns, regency stripes, covered them (never floral, that was non-U). The words toilet and toilet paper, ball-and-claw furniture, holding a knife between thumb and forefinger were non-U. The only swear words allowed were "bloody" and "bugger" and the word "kaffir" was comprehensively verboten.

The dogs and cats changed, but they all had long lives and the pattern in front of the granite fireplace continued over the years – half-circle of cats, half-circle of dogs. The servants stayed on the property: Emily Nyati who claimed to be a Swazi princess, and her husband Philemon, my father's chauffeur and Caroline Legae who replaced Stefalina but lived with us in the servants' quarters until the old girl and the old man moved from Oaklands to Norwood – the "village", Mom called it, and Anthony, the Malawian, who drove Mom around after her stroke. My father paid their wages in cash on the last Friday evening of the month at supper. When I was six in 1949, Emily received £10 a month. When she died, Judd, my brother, and his wife, Judy, were the only whites at the funeral arranged elaborately as part of her funeral insurance policies and held in Philemon's house in Hammanskraal, KwaNdebele, a sturdy and large brick house which he bought from his wages from HE Babb & Son from which he retired after 40 years, receiving a pension from Judd. What Emily taught me was Swazi, she insisted, but when I did a Zulu course, the vocabulary assimilated to Zulu.

If the suburban life went on its predictable course, what is there to describe? Joburg was not stuck in aspic. The arc of life brought with it an intriguing interplay during years when the microcosm of the world's salients and conflicts, South Africa, was blithely and comfortably populated with people as certain of their present as they were of their past. Of the future they were certain. Only once did my mother show some preoccupation when she was told by an artist friend, Kent Cottrell, that she had asked the gardener if he would kill her come the revolution. "No", he is reported to have said, "but the next-door gardener will". Mom related this half in jest, and gave it no further thought.

.Of the past, the genealogy was unchanging and definite. Mom had on her Dolly Varden, as she called her dressing table, large professional photographs of herself in long silk dresses. There were two themes: debutante with ivory-coloured shoes and ostrich feather boa, standing in profile with her borzoi at her side, dreamily staring into the distance, and wedding. She looks tall, though she was 5 ft 6 inches in her stockings. I stared at these black and white images long and often. It was so aspirational: she was going to be received at court. The photo was taken in Cape Town when she was seventeen, looking to me so mature, before sailing to Southampton in the Royal Holland Line ship. She does not get invited to the debutantes' ball.

She is summoned:

> *"The Lord Chamberlain is commanded by Their Majesties*
>
> *to summon Miss O.C. Loverock*
>
> *to a Court at Buckingham Palace*
>
> *on Tuesday the 12th June 1934*
>
> *at 9.30 o'clock p.m.*
>
> *Ladies: Court Dress with feathers and trains.*
>
> *Gentlemen: Full Court Dress."*

The silk wedding dress holds her slim body tightly. A coronet perches on her hair. She holds an enormous bouquet of arum lilies. The wedding photos show one of her bridesmaids holding it up triumphantly after catching it and the white ink caption reads: "The next to fall!" It is Dot Summers.

The social aspiration was less hers than her parents': her father, my grandfather, Cecil Victor Loverock, was born into an upper middle-class family. He attended Rugby School and his half-brother, Reginald, became housemaster at Harrow School. From what Mom said, Cecil was stern and disciplinarian. She said: "He just had to look at me over his glasses and say 'Ora!' and I was put in my place". Cecil Victor joined the panoply of framed photographs on the mantelshelf. He certainly looked stern. He watches the photographer carefully and looks straight into the lens. He is bald with a rim of dark hair. The glasses are rimless and round. You cannot tell the colour of his eyes, but they are light and, because his daughter and all his grandchildren have blue-grey eyes, they must have been the same. Everyone called him "Lovey". One photograph has him standing on the lawn at his house, *Borlumbeg*, in Tennant Street in Kenilworth, with a bald dome. There he looks vulnerable and, what doesn't emerge from other photographs, small.

Eric and Ora wedding

Aunt Maidie and Aunt Vi at Iverley House, Rugby

He had other half siblings born of his stepmother, Edith Bromwich. His own mother died while he was in his infancy and he was sent to live with an uncle, a Flynn. Two of his half-sisters, called Aunt Vi and Aunt Maidie, lived in the double storey house, Iverley House, with large garden they inherited from Cecil's father, Lewis. I corresponded enthusiastically with them as a boy and gave them our colonial news. They replied in their neat small handwriting: "What is a jalopy?" they asked, "What is a braai?" half-amused and forbearing of the childish presumption. They sent a photograph of the two of them sitting on the steps leading from the lawn, two grey-haired stick people with dresses half-way down their calves. When I went to Oxford, Mom took me to meet them. Prim. Polite. They served us tea in bone china with rose patterns on the cups and saucers. They used tongs to pick up the sugar cubes.

Loverock – a lark, in Scottish. The name taken by the Earl of Nithsdale on exile after consorting with Bonnie Prince Charlie. He is reputed to have smuggled into prison woman's clothing for the Prince to escape in. Family legend, and repeated by Mom often, held that we were descended from the Earl of Nithsdale and that Caerloverock Castle, a ruin, belonged to her as the oldest child of the direct descendent, Cecil. One of her great uncles had spent a eonsiderable time researching the family tree and had not been able to prove the descending line. It remained a dream, an aspiration, a confirmation of her appropriate genealogy. "Wayne," my elder brother, she said, "is rightly an Earl and owns a castle." That fairy tale was the stuff of legend and she dwelt on it fondly. It fixed her family in the constellation of the nobility.

Wayne studied the line of descent and has not turned up anything, beside the name, which would justify this fantasy. *Se non è vero, è ben trovato*. Who can dispute it?

What did come down from the Loverock genes, was an artistic bent. Yes: my grandfather had uncles who were members of the Royal Academy and passed on to Mom paintings by John Frederick Herring, John and James Faed, uncles to Cecil. Cecil's father, Lewis, mayor of

Rugby, married Annette Constance Herring, John Herring's sister, who died shortly after Cecil's birth at 24 years old. Herring's paintings of horses are legendary and still admired. It was as important then to have a portrait of your horses as of your family. My mother had horse prints hanging on the dining-room wall. One depicted a dog hanging on to the muzzle of a horse which read: "1st punter: 'It's a 10L horse'; 2nd punter: 'This'll make him a 5L horse!'" The painting remnants of the Scottish Loverocks hang in my house after adorning the large sitting-room of 17 Park Street, Oaklands, for all the years of our youth together with a large Dutch convex mirror (a looking glass!) in a gold frame. Both Mom, who attended the Michaelis School of Art, and my sons, St John and Edward, have the deft hands and the imagination of these forebears.

One of John Faed's watercolours depicts a manager or a clerk in his cottage, a hand to his forehead, while a bonneted lady, serves him a plate of food at a fine circular table. Alongside stands a cot in which a chubby sleeping baby is swaddled in cream blankets. A blue knitted sock lies on the floor. "What is the sex of the baby?" Mom asked, and the detective in us had to identify the sock as belonging to a boy. The watercolour is atmospheric and dreamy. I looked and looked at it and gave it its own backstory. Another is a pencil sketch of a winklepicker by John. Faed had a wryness because the drawing is from behind and the basket, the floppy hat and the back of the boots make the prime focus of the drawing. The

Lewis Loverock and Constance Herring

Cecil Victor Loverock: "Lovey"

third is a watercolour by James Faed of a young woman, hair swept back, sewing a tapestry on her knees seated on the edge of a Sheraton chair, eyes downcast. To find the signatures on these pictures, you need to seek odd places, like the crossbar of the chair, to find the tiny admission of responsibility, a sign of modesty.

Cecil Victor, after Rugby School, joined the Eastern Telegraph Company. The telegraph and telephone exemplified the new technology, the IT of the time and an exciting venture in modern communication science. It was a profitable and growing industry – a telegram once cost a pound a word. The Eastern Telegraph Company had the concession to lay the telegraph cables though Europe from Lisbon, through Trieste and down the East coast of Africa via Zanzibar and Delagoa Bay in Portuguese East Africa, to Durban and Cape Town.

The young Cecil Victor Loverock became station chief in Gibraltar, then the company transferred him to Durban and then Cape Town. In the Cape, he moved in the circles of the old monied Capetonians, the Spilhauses, the Bertishes, the Rose-Inneses, the Ovenstones and the Garlicks. These were the families that provided the bridesmaids for my mother's wedding. From the only letter I possess written by Lovey, addressed to my father, starting with "My dear Old Eric." His sentences are peppered with "old chap", "old fellow" and "old man", the form of affectionate address of the public school. He was in the up-and-coming industry of the moment and like a fish in water.

From Durban, he moved to the corporate compound in Barrack Street in the centre of Cape Town and then rented a property in the affluent suburb of Kenilworth. In 1911, he married the girl who was deemed the Beauty of Cape Town, Nina Italia Doering. It is difficult for me to imagine her as the "Beauty of Cape Town". In a sepia print before her wedding, she looks fetchingly and romantically over her shoulder. At her wedding she wore an elaborate peasant bouffant flounced full-length dress holding a large bouquet of flowers and wearing a pudding mould hat. Other pictures I have date from after my mother, Ora Constance's, birth, showing a Junoesque robustness and a heavy jawline.

As she grew frail, she came to live with us at 17 Park Street and it was not the best time to judge her life. The early photographs show a heavy-jawed woman, dressed at first in half-calf dresses, then the twenties fashion of the flappers, cloche hat and bobbed hair, usually pictured with my mother who sported a huge silk bow in her dark (she called it "mousey") hair and short white socks. Mom was born in 1913. On Lovey's death Nina inherited £1840 and a Ford sedan valued at £100. She moved to *Wittebome*, a lovely estate on Constantia Main Road and, then, later, a flat in *Schoongezicht*, a block of apartments in Main Road, Kenilworth. An avid letter writer, I sent my missives there.

When Grannie Nina, in her dotage, lived with us, her breasts had flattened to pancakes and the chest was covered with cotton dresses that stretched down to her calves. She wore tortoise-shell eyeglasses and her false teeth clicked constantly, of which she seemed to be wholly unaware. She smoked interminably. Her faded memory brought little enlightenment to us. She said she gave 'good advice' to girls at dances: "Smile, it makes you look so much better". She was a puzzle to Mandy and us boys. She did not seem to read, though she did knit. Mom asked us to keep her occupied, so Wayne and I asked her to knit us each a college scarf, one in blue the other in maroon, the school colours. We did not say so, but we were happy when the garage was converted into a cottage for her, though she ate each evening at our table. A dull presence. No spark. Staring without inquisitiveness into the distance,

Nina and Lovey

living out her last days under the aegis of her sole daughter. She had had a son, Lawrence, named after her brother, who died after a few days. So, let's cut her a bit of slack.

Then came the First World War. I have a photograph of Cecil in a uniform, but he did not go to the European front – he was despatched to Delagoa Bay and then Zanzibar. Neighbouring Tanganyika was then a German colony where General Smuts was pursuing the German commander, Paul von Lettow-Vorbeck with troops struck down by malaria, dysentery and malnutrition. The posting of a telegraph specialist, like my grandfather, to nearby Zanzibar could only have been an intelligence operation to track the German communications. This will explain why the uniform does not feature again. He had also, according to company records,   attended "special short courses" in England in 1914 and 1917 which makes the deduction that he was involved in intelligence operations plausible.

Ora Constance Loverock, our Mom

Mom's snaps from Zanzibar are an excited assembly of exotica. Arabs in kaftans and turbans, tribal reunions, coconut trees and big white official residences. Inevitably there is the nanny carrying Ora on her back. In Ora's impeccably assembled and neatly annotated stamp album, there is a page of an unfranked full set of Zanzibari stamps featuring the sheik in a handsome central cartouche.

After the first war, Cecil Victor was posted to Dar-es-Salaam and back to Cape Town as managing director with full responsibility for the Eastern Telegraph's telecommunications. Mom said he was the fastest morse code sender in the world. During the thirties, the Eastern Telegraph company merged with the concessionary on Africa's west coast and became Cable & Wireless. Lovey became joint managing director of the new firm covering almost all South Africa' telegraphic and wireless communication. During the Second World War, the international traffic on the wireless and telegraph service increased exponentially. My mother believed that the war killed him. Lovey died of overwork when he had a cardiac arrest in 1943 at age 59. The memorial book of his funeral lists 94 wreaths and bouquets sent by the élite families for his cremation at Maitland cemetery.

My grandparents had sent my mother to St Cyprian's College in Oranjezicht. This was near where my great-grandparents, Charles Homer Doering and Ora senior lived at Mackinaw House in Forest

Lovey at Tennant Rd, Kensington, Cape Town

Avenue in Oranjezicht. I imagine that Cecil and Nina moved in with them for them to have chosen St Cyprian's, the foremost girls' Anglican School in Cape Town. The photograph of Charles Homer and Ora on the top balcony of Mackinaw House shows Ora senior as slim, bespectacled and austere. She has a receding jawline. It is 1916 and a large canvas-roofed sedan is parked outside the house. Some of the photos depict them holding Ora junior tentatively at arm's length, Charles Homer in a high lapelled jacket and Ora senior wearing the inevitable ankle-length cotton dress and round spectacles. On the back of the photo great-grannie Ora has written: "Don't I look fat and inelegant."

In contrast to her severe exterior, I detect a sense of humour and an iron-fisted attitude, including tough love and discipline. She recounted how she had ridden back from Charles Homer's practice in Johannesburg and was surprised that the horse slowed down and stopped. Puzzled, she looked around. The horse had stopped at a tavern, where it usually waited for Charles Homer. This happened a second time at another inn. She recounted this amicably in conversation. She was more amused than admonishing. Her comments annotated on the back of photos she sent of their stock farm, also showed a wryness. On the back of one: "This is me brudder. He has a bigger nose than me." You can hear her pride as she describes the barn on the reverse of a photo of the Allison Stock Farm the Doerings, my great-grandparents, had bought in Ontario. "The part on the left of the tower has 64 stalls for cows. The right is the stable for the horses." A photograph of fat Frisians with tags in the ears filling all the stalls follows. The double storey house she describes with pleasure

Allison Dairy Farm, Chesterville, Ontario

on the back of its photo: the study, the main bedroom, the dining room.

Then came the unhappiest period in my mother's life. A girl who had ridden horses through the forests of Pinelands, dug sandcastles on Muizenberg beach and played tennis at St Cyprian's found herself on the ship to Southampton on a Royal Netherlands ship headed for Roedean School in Brighton, England. Cecil Victor wanted to show the superiority of English education and the English upper class over the restricted colonials. This pandering to the English essence percolated through Mom's life. Taste, language and mores were dictated by England. It would be a mitigating circumstance of her Roedean confinement if it coincided with a short stint Cecil had in Portugal, in 1927.

This miserable time for Mom is summed up in a single tale of this grey schooling. The school was walking in a crocodile on Sunday outside Brighton when some horse riders passed them. Mom said loudly: "Lucky beggars!" for which she was gated for four weeks. She presumed the teacher had heard "Lucky buggers!" one of the few swearwords we were allowed in the house. This incident stung her for the rest of her life, but hardly had an impact on her conviction of the greatness of England and the English. And her insistence that we all speak the King's English, round our vowels and not drop our "t's". No glottal stops. We children all got used to having our sentences corrected and our accents primed.

Such was the Anglophone love affair, that my father and mother were part of the enthusiastic band that cheered the Royal Visit in 1947. This did not please all of Afrikanerdom. When the Royal cortège visited Cape Town, *Die Burger* warned Capetonians sourly not to venture to Adderley Street as there would be heavy traffic there. No word about the Royal Visit was published in *Die Burger* or *Die Transvaler,* whose editor was Hendrik Verwoerd. Clarendon Circle in Joubert Park was deprived of its cannas and a huge, illuminated crown was built over the circle. My parents had even booked an apartment on Hospital Hill to see the royal family pass and shared the balcony with friends. Shortly before their appearance, I held my groin and said: "I want to wee-wee." Crossly, Mom took me to the lav and was back in time. I could see through the pillars of the balcony how a patient in a wheelchair wheeled himself to the middle of the road to block the cortège. Police, wardens and the public wheeled him back quickly to the pavement. The apartment was opposite the General Hospital and patients in hospital gowns lined the road. It was all over in a flash with much screaming and delighted cries and whistles and waving of little Union Jacks. Mom and Dad took the blue Chev and the Stewarts and headed off for Basutoland to watch it all over again. One of Mom's flames, Brian Marwick, was at the High Commissioner's office and he had arranged seats for them to see another parade, this time led by Basotho ponies. They got through the border post late so slept in sleeping bags next to the road. Mom said they discovered in the light of day that their comfortable bed was a dung heap.

On her return from Roedean, Mom went to the Michaelis School of Art in Orange Street. She must have also been to a secretarial school, too, because she could touch type on her portable Royal typewriter that pounded out small letters. These small letters have remained on the recipe cards she typed and kept neatly in a small index box in the kitchen. There the recipes are: Ham Cooked in Beer; Salmon Mousse; Melting Moments; Heaven's Broth. She did not ever mention getting "A" levels or school-leaving certificates, so university would not have been her destination.

If one were a "what-iffer?" one could design multiple potential paths for Mom. She had a deft hand and could have evolved into a competent, imaginative artist. When, after her stroke, she produced a stunning large pastel of white roses on a green background, I could only gape and wonder what she could have achieved if he had stayed with painting and art instead of 35 bourgeois housewifery years. Too little of what she was capable of remains: a circular brown pencil drawing of a cavalier on a prancing horse, her wry take of a cartoon series of a bloodhound following a bug to its hole and then walking away its nose in the air which adorns my autograph book and another cartoon of a hunter, sweating, too tired to shoot the lion. She obviously did not get any encouragement from Cecil and Nina who fixated on her joining the establishment, marrying and becoming a solid burgher's wife.

At Michaelis School of Art, she met a lifelong friend, Mullie Borchers, who like many of Mom's friends had obvious Malay antecedents with the popular names of the time - Ardrienne becoming Mickey, Muriel becoming Mullie, Winifred becoming Winnie, Ivy staying Ivy. Mullie, too, stopped her art career on marrying Dr Rupert Borchers, the geologist who discovered the Welkom ridge of the Southern goldfields. The ceramic woman in diaphanous clothes draped over the grey form of a hippopotamus she had fired, lived with the Borchers in all their abodes – this was all she had to show from her years at Michaelis. From the photos, the art school came second to the circle of friends in their sports jackets, flannels and open-topped cars. The smart set spent their time on car rallies and at the golf course and leaned nonchalantly against the bonnet of the Packard, Willy's or Chevrolet. The aspiration was American.

After the geological discovery of gold near Welkom, Rupert (Bill) and Mullie lived for three months in a caravan in the driveway of 17 Park Street. It was here that they asked Mom and Dad become foster parents to their children, Valerie and Jeremy. This constituted great confidence in my parents' stability. They both signed the undertakings on our dining room table. I witnessed this and was inwardly moved that children could be entrusted to others with such faith and belief.

Amongst the young Cape set was my father. He wore his hair with an almost centre parting. "He was so handsome," my mother said, "I said to myself I'd marry him." And she did. Steps Rowe, whose mother was Mom's godmother, exclaimed indignantly: "Why is she throwing herself away on a mere travelling salesman?" Mom said of herself: "I am no oil painting" but she had 36" breasts. She complained that she had had to bind them in. She called her nose "a Roman nose" as it bent at the bridge. She was slim and she was witty and spoke well. It was a society wedding, all right. From St Saviour's Anglican Church, the party with four bridesmaids from the monied families of Cape Town went to Kelvin Grove Club for the wedding breakfast. I was told that my father was so nervous that his speech consisted of: "I am the moon, and she is my sun." (I later wondered how he became chairman of UKSATA, the UK-South Africa Trade Association, the British Manufacturers' Representatives Association and the Old Johannian Association when he was such a nervous and hesitant public speaker.) The newspapers dedicated many column inches to the event and photos appeared in *The Cape Argus* and *The Cape Times* of my mother and her bridesmaids and guests from the great and the good of Cape Town. My mother bears a bouquet of arum lilies which appears in the studio wedding photo on her dressing table.

This was the time when Horace Edwin, Dad's father, closed down the Cape Town office. It was also the time when Horace had remarried. After his first wife, Maude's, death, he had gone on an ocean cruise and met Margaret Padwick on board. My mother was convinced that Peggy, as she was called, had ensnared Horace into marrying this ascetic and aggressive spinster, on the shelf at 38. He was 62, vulnerable and on the rebound from the death of his beloved Maude. On 1 September 1939 they married in Kensington, London. They must have just missed the lockdown at the beginning of the Second World War for they married on the very day Germany invaded Poland. Great Britain declared war two days later.

Peggy remained an enigma. No warmth streamed out of her. She had gimlet eyes. Her skin made her look like a stick of biltong. My mother only spoke disparagingly of her cynicism. It looked as though Peggy haughtily regarded the Babb children as lower order colonials. She was an aggressive and bellicose woman, epitomised by a tight bun behind her head. She joined up with the SPCA (or the Royal Society as it then was) but found the management pathetic and not to her liking, so she founded a competing body, the People's Dispensary for Sick Animals. Hugh, my cousin, accompanied her on her raids into Alexandra township where she caught all the stray dogs she could. If she could find the owners, she berated them for their treatment of their pets and gave them a lecture on what to do. If the dogs were ill, Peggy condemned them to a quick death. Hugh had to do the catching. "Get that one!" she cried.

She had a malign influence on Horace. In the letter of advice Lovey writes in 1940 to my father in which he regularly refers to Peggy, he says that Henry Rose-Innes states that there was no contractual relation between Pop (Horace) and Eric, my father, except that of employer and employee. There was no business partnership. Peggy had induced Pop to take control of the partnership and solely deal with the several principals, Arrow Shirts, Cannon Towels, Baltimore Hats, Beacon blankets, BVD underwear, Braemar knitwear and Wain Shiell suiting and fabric. Lovey wrote that nothing prevented Dad from starting a new agency but doubted that the principals would follow him if they knew there was dispute in the firm and advises that Dad waits for Pop's death. He took that advice, but Pop lived to eighty-nine. We never got beyond the lawn if we visited Horace with Dad and I never saw the inside of my grandfather's house in Waverley. Peggy hovered around like a bad-tempered prefect. I do not think she ever addressed a word to me at all. I do not think that Horace knew our names. If I went to HE Babb & Son's office in Bradlow's Building, von Brandis Street, Horace was mostly away, but if he was there he was ill-tempered and resented my taking used postage stamps from the big tin he kept them in for the Rotary Club, of which he became Governor from Nairobi to Cape Town. I stared at his bushy eyebrows that stuck out from his forehead. A sign on his desk read: "Is it good? Is it nice? Is it necessary to repeat it?" Another tin lay on the windowsill overlooking the blank wall of the next-door building. This tin contained seed for the pigeons which cooed and pecked at his closed window. Every day at work, he wore a red carnation in his lapel. Since I only ever saw him in a suit, it always had a carnation in the buttonhole.

Horace and Peggy sailed for South Africa and as their ship docked in Cape Town, Hugh, my father Eric's younger brother, shot himself in the offices of HE Babb and Sons. His suicide remained a puzzle. I have only met one person in Cape Town who knew Hugh, at that time, a frail old lady in her nineties. She said: "He was such a lovely man. He was a man of film star handsomeness. Why would he do that? None of us understood. He was so young. All of us loved him and wanted to be with him. Nobody knows why." In the family the suicide was raised only in hushed tones and everyone skated quickly over it. Two of the next generation, nevertheless, got his name, my brother, Judson Hugh, and my cousin, Dad's sister's son, Hugh.

In 2010, I received an e-mail from Hoey Pietersen. He had seen my e-mail address in a report, attached to the name Babb. Hoey was born in 1939, had children who were deceased as were his parents and he was alone in the world. His father was Hugh Babb, and he also bore the name Hugh, but no-one in his community could pronounce or even knew such a name, so he was called Hoey. He had a box of letters, photos and mementoes about Hugh he wanted to show me. How I wanted to meet this man! Could I not invite him to our house and fetch him? He declined as he was going for an operation and we could get together after that. Silence ensued. I sent several e-mails to him until one elicited a response. It came from the matron of the home where Hoey had been staying. She was sorry to let me know that Hoey had passed away. He had not recovered from the operation. She did not know what had happened to the box of letters. Hoey was clearly a Coloured man. I knew nothing of his life. He just declared that Hugh Babb was his father. No other person in Cape Town than my uncle could have borne that name. This gave a tenuous clue as to why Hugh had topped himself – he had made a Coloured woman pregnant and the great and good of Cape Town and his father would not forgive him or allow him back into polite company. He only saw one way out. The worst one.

The Cape Town office closed down. My father and mother with their new-born, Wayne, moved to Johannesburg. The cycle was completed. Mom returned to where her grandfather had started his dental practice in South Africa. Nina's father, Charles Homer Doering, had joined his uncle, Frederick in the first dental practice in Joburg. Charles Homer was born in 1866 in Wellesley, Waterloo, Ontario. He studied dentistry at the Philadelphia Dental School and married the first Ora, Ora Patterson. He spent ten years in Oregon before moving to Johannesburg in 1898, where his uncle, Frederich had set up his practice as a dentist. Frederich had been in Johannesburg some time and had treated the Jameson Raiders' teeth. He lived the good life and moved in the circles that dictated Joburg's social life.

This completes another nicely closed circle because I was assigned as ambassador of South Africa to Canada in 1985 and so went back to the roots of my mother's family. I regret now not having made more of the Doering connection because Charles Homer and Ora had purchased the Allison Stock farm in Chesterville, Ontario. Like Horace, he was a freemason and rose swiftly through the ranks and was given full masonic honours at his funeral in 1932. He was balloted on 14 August 1911 and initiated in the Southern Cross lodge and within four months was raised to the "sublime degree of Master Mason on 11 December 1911" – a meteoric rise.

His uncle, Frederich, the head of the dental practice, consorted with the elite of Johannesburg. Mentioned in one of his obituaries, is a bridge game where he partnered General Louis Botha against Sir Thomas Cullinan and Sir George Farrar and won a handsome sum from the two randlords. General Botha took Frederich with him to help him buy two merino rams with the winnings since they both had farms at Standerton. Louis Botha had made possible Frederich's purchase of his farm. He called the rams "Thomas" and "George" after the randlords he had trimmed. General Botha was a progressive and committed farmer. (This word appears on the plinth under his statue in front of Parliament: "Statesman. Warrior. Farmer.") It intrigued me that a passport application form of another Prime Minister, Hendrik Verwoerd, which I rescued from the shredding machine at the Union Buildings also gives that Prime Minister's profession as farmer: "Beroep: BOER", it reads. In his diary during the Versailles Treaty 1919 preparations, Louis Botha wrote that he took time off to go to Rambouillet north of Paris, where the best merino stud farms were. He recounts how the stud farmer showed contempt on seeing this outlandish Boer – a *"takhaar"* or hayseed. When Botha said he wanted to buy three rams, the manager dismissively replied: "Choose the three you want," and wandered off. Botha writes in Dutch that when he returned with his three choices, the supervisor checked the brandmarks on the horns in the studbook and blanched: "Those are my best rams!" Botha writes: "*Toen het ik mij op mijn schouder geklop en vir mijnself geseg: 'Hotnot'!*" which I roughly translate as: "Then I patted myself on my shoulder and said to myself: 'Bloody good show'!"

The Boer War broke out in 1899 and the Charles Homer Doerings with Nina, our grandmother, decamped to Durban where Charles Homer treated military personnel before moving to Bloemfontein where he provided dental services for the British army. In his obituary, the obituarist refers to war service during the Boer War. This must relate to his employment by the British Army as a medical officer. He took his family, which consisted of twins, Vernon and Lawrence, and Nina, back to Joburg before the end of the war, in 1901, where he worked for the military again. The twins, little blond boys, identical, look inquisitively at the camera. Vernon died of diphtheria in 1902. Lawrence was sent to St John's Preparatory School when it still had classes at the tin shack at the Union Grounds and he stands with big ears at the back edge of the class.

His great uncle, Frederich, had by then departed for Kenya where the British were promoting immigration and the next we hear from him is a rambling letter dated 29 November 1939 addressed to his niece, Barbara Doering, from his home in Jersey before German occupation of the Channel Islands. This missive, hard to read and composed over several days, lays into Lawrence as a lazy ne'er-do-well who continually asks him for money. He wonders if Lawrence has touched the folk in Chesterville, Canada, where Charles Homer had ended up, for a loan. He complains that the newspapers are feeding him "mush" and says he always believed the Germans were "honest and truthfull (*sic*)" but now under Hitler they are "theives (*sic*)". When, after German occupation, he gets a response through the Red Cross from Barbara **(strictly no more than 40 words)** he says this is the first ray of light in three years.

Charles Homer applied to the Transvaal Colonial Secretary to be admitted as a Joburg dental practitioner, for which he had failed to register before the Boer War. He was refused as the new Colony did not accept USA degrees. He appealed and after consultation, he was permitted to practise but under the Transvaal Proclamation Section 2 he could not have his name placed on the Dentists' Register. In Minute 9265/02 of 29 April 1903, the Assistant Colonial Secretary writes: "It is held, however, that as Dr Doering was in practice as a Dentist in the Transvaal prior to the war, he is entitled, under Section 2 of the Proclamation, to continue to practise without his name being placed on the Dentists' Register of the Colony."

By 1906 he had moved to Oranjezicht, Cape Town, and practised dentistry again in Cape Town until he left the country in 1923 to return to Canada where he bought the Allison stock farm. His daughter, Nina Italia, had married Lovey and had moved to Kenilworth.

Eric, my father was born in Cardiff, Wales, on 13 April 1913, just six months before my mother's birth in Cape Town. Horace, his father, and his wife Maude Ware, moved in 1914 shortly before the First World War, to Cape Town. His marriage certificate describes him as a "master draper" and the 1901 census describes Horace's father in turn as a coach builder or cabinet maker. Horace had lived in Barnstaple, Devonshire, at 29 Sticklepath Terrace. He had a sister and four brothers. He received his indenture as a draper in 1891 when he was a mere 14 years old.

Dr Charles Homer Doering

It requires him not to "play at Cards or Dice Tables" and not to enter matrimony "for the Term of the Apprenticeship" of five years and not to "waste the Goods of his said Master" and to "behave himself towards the said Master." All of this for four shillings a week "for the Term of the Apprenticeship."

He spent his youth years driving cars. Car manufacturers employed him at the end of the nineteenth century. The motoring correspondent, Paul Irwin, of *The Star* wrote in his obituary:

"One of the world's earliest motorists – he got his British driving licence in 1899 – Mr Babb designed and built a convertible sedan in 1902.

"The idea came to him when he was employed to tour Britain by car to prove that motoring had come to stay.

"He was given, as he once said: 'a mechanised surrey with a fringe on the top.' It was totally unsuited to the British weather, so he fitted it with a glass-windowed steel top which was held in place by eight bolts and could be taken off when the sun shone.

"When Mr Babb visited the United States in 1918 and chatted with a group of car executives about his early motoring days, one American said: 'What do you know? We've been kidding ourselves we built the sedan in 1910 – but this guy beat us by eight years.' It was while touring Britain in 1902 that Mr Babb ... was summoned for reckless driving. He was fined £2 3s and

Mackinaw House, Oranjezicht: Great-grandparents Charles Homer, Ora senior and Grannie Nina and Mom, Ora

his licence was endorsed by the Reading Magistrate because he was travelling at more than 12 miles per hour."

The name Babb is prevalent in the West of England and Devonshire. Most of the Babbs I have met have been West Indian black people who had come to Canada. As West Country people, some Babbs had, I guess, started plantations in the West Indies where it was custom that slaves would take their master's name. I love the name. When asked to spell it, I add: "The first two letters of the alphabet, one of them three times."

HE Babb & Son, which had started out as HE Babb & Sons, set up shop in Bradlow's Buildings, von Brandis Street, Joburg above the furniture merchants, Bradlow's, competitors to Geen & Richards. The office was on the fourth floor via an Otis lift with trellis doors which you had to slam closed to ensure it could be called to another floor. In France, the expression "*renvoyer moi l'ascenseur*", or pay me back a favour, always raised the image of this slow-moving box. A flat, polished brass handrail ran round the interior. Beware of the thing: do not put your tiny fingers behind it because one of the brothers will squeeze them against the side by leaning on the handrail. In the office on the fourth floor sat Mrs Ollver, fat, short, silent and very short-sighted. Very, very short-sighted. When she typed a letter, she raised the draft right to her pebble glasses and put it down before recommencing and peering at the typed page. She stayed at that desk throughout my youth and was dutifully at her post for forty-odd years. On the shelves stood the samples of towels, blankets, shirts, hats, sheets, fabric and, stacked against the wall, were the skips.

Skips were the major tool for agents and representatives. They measured three feet by three feet by four feet, were made of cane or wicker and had two clasps for the padlocks. The skips accompanied the agents on their trips to Durban, Port Elizabeth, East London and Cape Town. Agents got together and arranged a display of their goods at an hotel to which they bade their clients to examine the newest and best and to place their orders. The skips, filled with merchandise, went by freight train and the agents' assistants fetched them from the porters' trolleys at the railway stations and lugged them to the display room at the hotel. The same Indian doorman had always been at the Royal Hotel in Durban and when we were on a family visit to Durban, greeted my father like a long-lost friend, a decade after this marketing practice ended.

In the office there was a hat stretcher. Two half cylinders were wound apart by a handle and you stretch a hat from 7 to 7¼. We knew all the sizes. The brothers all had 16-inch collars, 36-inch waists, size 7 heads. Since the samples from Arrow were 16-inch, this made clothing us less burdensome for the family finances. The linen, towels, blankets and pillowcases at home consisted of the post-season samples. Arrow shirts, which were famous for never losing their buttons, appear in Cole Porter's song, *You're the Top*:

> "You're the top! You're an Arrow collar!
> You're the top! You're a Coolidge dollar!"

So, Grandpop had secured the top end of the imported clothing and fabric market.

On the ground floor of the same building were two shops we visited Mr Tuck's shoe shop for school shoes, and the barber. The smell of the new leather and glue was intoxicating. Tuck's shop was narrow, and shoeboxes stretched up on the shelves to the ceiling. In the middle stood public works green chairs with a footstool to try on the shoes. If Dad were not in the office or visiting clients, we could find him here, chatting to Mr Tuck. Tuck and Dad discussed horse-racing tips. Next door was the barber. The barber put a plank over the arm rests to be able to reach the heads of the boys, who, like *Cheaper by the Dozen*, were tonsured together.

My mother and father moved to Joburg just as the Second World War began. That my father could not join the other young men who volunteered in droves to go "up North", scarred him forever. The young men wore the orange shoulder patch, *"die rooi lissie"*, that showed that they had volunteered to fight outside South Africa. The old man had already, in July 1933, received an "Exemption from Military Service on Medical Grounds" in terms of the South Africa Defence Act 1912 having volunteered for national service: "Eric Ware Babb ...is exempt from Peace Training or from service in a Rifle Association, he having been pronounced by the prescribed military authority as unfit for military service in any capacity", signed by Officer Commanding No. 4 Military District. When a teenager at St John's, after a boxing bout, he had collapsed from his bicycle on his way home and was hospitalised for rheumatic fever. This excluded him from enjoying the camaraderie of the forces. All he could do was become a member of the Civic Guard. He received a medal for his service which he shyly kept in a drawer next to his bed. Being a member of the Civic Guard entailed doing night shifts of patrolling the streets of Joburg. He stopped two Black men running up 11th Avenue in Houghton: "Shit cart boys, baas!", they said and sped on. Lumbering up the hill behind them came the night soil wagon drawn by two horses with eye flaps. The sewage system had not reached all Joburg's suburbs and little sanitary lanes for the deposit of ordure stretched out from major roads. My mother volunteered as an ambulance driver and described with horror the wounds of the soldiers flown back from Egypt to South Africa. "The boys in tanks suffered the most," she said, "burns and wounds at the same time." The disappointment was immense for my father on missing out on this adventure, because adventure is what the Springboks, as the soldiers were called, deemed it to be.

Mom and Dad's war effort extended also to taking in RAF officers who stayed in our house. Mom was amused that the *Encyclopaedia of Sex* attracted the officers' attention more than any other book in the bookcases. She said she put it back on the shelf upside down just for the fun of finding it back upright when she next saw it. It was an obstetrician's handbook and displayed coloured dissections of wombs and fallopian tubes. No titillation there – the title was highly misleading.

One of the lodgers became an RAF wing commander. He had made a big impression on her. She remained in contact with him long after the war – the sort of man with a position which would have suited her social aspirations. My parents also gave comfort to Daggie and Ernest Lenning who owned a steel works in Joburg. At outbreak of war, Ernest, a German, was interned as an enemy alien. They knew one another socially and in business circles. Together with their friends, the Stewarts, they drove out to their smallholding at Meyerton almost every weekend. All they could offer was moral support and friendship to Daggie because none of them knew how to candle an egg or pitch hay. The Smuts government would have done better to arrest the clerics in Napier in the Cape who were sending messages to German submarines from the Dutch Reformed Church tower.

The Stewarts cashed in their chips with the Lennings later. Mickey persuaded Daggie to pay for their daughter, Jean, to attend finishing school in Switzerland for a year. Jeremy Taylor sang of a finishing school in one of his South African ballads: *"And that finishing school finished her klaar"* which was the sad fate of Jean ending as an alcoholic married to one.

A couple of years after the war, my father took Wayne and me to a rally on Union Day at Zoo Lake. The fireworks which shot Daniel Malan's image into the air led to a violent disruption by the Springbok Legion, an organisation of ex-servicemen led by Communists like Joe Slovo, Jack Hodgson (whom my parents knew and who was an explosives expert) and Fred Carneson whose overt aims were anti-racist but who were covertly ideologically extreme left wing. In 1951, it transmogrified into the Torch Commando which arranged night-time torch marches through all the towns in South Africa, comparing the National Party to the Nazis and demanding that the Coloureds not be removed from the common voters' roll. The Afrikaans press referred to them as the "*Blikfakkels*" in reference to the tins of burning oil that the marchers, on one occasion numbering 75,000 in Durban, held on sticks. It was at the apogee of its popularity when the Coloureds were at last removed from the voters' roll by political trickery in 1951. The Torch Commando had the financial and political support of Harry Oppenheimer MP and Sailor Malan, the flying ace. Frightened of our being trampled underfoot during the mayhem, Dad gathered us up and fled to the car. "But the fireworks haven't finished yet!" we indignantly cried. Nevertheless, Dad bought a torch commando pin which the members wore when they went on the torchlight marches.

On arrival in Joburg, my parents bought a two-acre rambling house in Oaklands. It had been the stables of the next-door home. Mom was delighted to find an old saddle secreted in the ceiling. Oaklands was the outlier suburb to classy Houghton and, already in the nineteenth century, Victorian piles had risen in the suburb. Opposite us, on Park Street was a red brick double storey with stables and a decorative steeple, owned by Old Man Martin, the founder of Swan Press. There were still bullet holes in it from the Boer War when a patrol had opened fire on a light after curfew. The architect was English, so the house faced South where the architect thought the sunlight came from. The conservatory was on the wrong side of the building and no plants or seedlings could survive there. In the large dining-room a candelabra lamp with several arms hung over the table. Each time the family ate chicken, the wishbone was hung over the chandelier. The macabre decoration got more elaborate and dustier over the year, but at Christmas, the wishbones were all taken down and pulled with the wishes for the next year. We only knew Mr Martin in his old age. Each

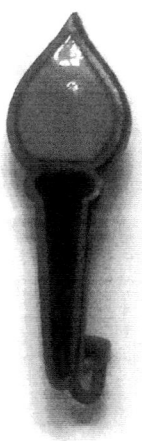

The Torch Commando pin

evening he shuffled, stooped, walking stick in hand, black coat hanging below his knees, with his black Labrador, around the block – down Park Street, left into Stella Street, left into Meyer Street and left again into African Street back to Park Street. The dog began to walk slower and slower, its head hanging ever less proudly, its black tail dragging behind it. When the Labrador died, old man Martin did not last two weeks. He was issue of the Victorian age in the Dickensian sense of the word. Two of his unmarried daughters lived with him. One, Jean, who was already in her fifties, hardly had he died, took off for Kenya to meet up with the flame of her youth, whom Martin had prevented her from marrying. Well, that fire was not lit again, and Jean was back within six months, still unmarried and sadder than ever.

In the centre of the next block, another improbable mansion, double storey, red brick with stucco edging and two towers and crenellations, rose imposingly out of the veld. Trees lined a driveway to the front door, but the real entrance was in Haswell Street through a high red brick arch which made up part of the stables. In our teenagehood, the block was broken up into smaller plots, one of which was bought by the Todd family into which my brother, Judson, married. And some Philistines razed old man Martin's house and built a non-descript ranch house in its place. All that remained was the deodar tree of a hundred feet on the croquet lawn. The stables were kept as servants' quarters.

Deodars lined the drive up to our house. *Cedrus deodara*, the cedar from the Himalayas. Mom mouthed the botanical name lovingly. The trees grew with us and, by the time I left home, they were 70 feet high. Two lower branches were wired together to form our annual Christmas tree. Twelve trees down one side and ten on the other as the drive curved round to the house.

The house, formerly the stables of the house next door, owned by the Serruriers; he, a Western Province cricketer, she, sister of Roger Bushell, the leader of the Great Escape, shot by the Nazis. The stables had been extended and a wide stoep stretched across its front. Incongruously, the house was plastered in a Spanish stucco with generous trowels of undulating plaster. The house was far from Park Street and flanked on our western neighbours, the Goldbergs. The garden was two acres in size with a downward sloping wide lawn below and a flatter lawn in front of the stoep. Because of the sloping lawn, Mom wanted to call the house "Meadowbank", but the sign was never made, and Dad never erected the white picket fence she so wanted on Park Street. The ceilings were covered with pressed steel panels, patterned differently in each room. The sitting room was thirty-two feet long and halfway along, an immense grey granite fireplace with a big grate provided the centrepiece to our family life. Above it hung Mom's Dutch convex mirror. The roof, like the overwhelming number in Joburg, was made of corrugated iron, painted black. The rain danced and pinged on it and when it hailed, you could not speak loud enough to be heard.

At 15, my troubled teenage critical faculties deemed that the house was shabby. I persuaded the old man that I could paint it, or rather whitewash it, because whitewash was under the dust. The house had not been painted in my 15 years. The roof was peeling. Dad offered me £5 for the job. Bob a job. Norwood Hardware, where he held an account, would provide the materials. I struggled up the hill to the village on my bike and struggled back again with a couple of bags of whitewash powder to mix, and a wide whitewash brush. We only had a short stepladder, so I had to climb onto the stoep roof and paint the upper bits of the walls from above, lying on the tin roof with my feet above me. I mixed buckets of whitewash and mounted the roof. It was agony. Pain. Whitewash stings the eyes. It makes them red. It chafes and hurts your skin. By the second day I was in overalls and wearing my wide underwater goggles backed with black rubber. Judd and Wayne laughed, teased and mocked me and did not offer to help. My temper was frayed. I had been conned, I thought. "But you offered!" they laughed. I had. I could foresee my July holiday entirely occupied by this achingly painful job. By dint of stretching to my highest from the ladder and leaning as far as I could over the gutters, the whole big house was whitewashed. Except a patch below the eastern gable which

I could not reach even with the brush tied by rope to a broom handle. Then came the messier part. The roof paint needed to be a bitumen black which stuck and clung to everything. The overalls slowly turned almost entirely black. Turpentine did not clean my hands even with a scrubbing brush. The tar stuck in my hair and spotted my face. I fell off the roof twice, on both occasions into the apricot tree behind the porch which partially broke my fall. For the corrugated iron, you needed a special roller with indentations to match the corrugations. I had to ride three times to Norwood Hardware to replace the rollers which had fossilised with the tar, to the amusement of Mr Chambers who owned the shop. I just hoped Dad had paid his account so I could replenish the supplies. I did a good job, but the patch under the eastern gable plagued me till I left home years later. The bare bit was never whitewashed and always stared accusingly at me when I came up the drive. It was the first thing I could see on arrival, and I grumbled to myself inwardly.

Dad uttered no praise, which was not in his character, but I did receive my £5 and had a week of holiday left to spend it on stamps from Hollings Philately in Plein Street.

The house had four bedrooms, so Juddy and I had to share, as we were two years apart. Two single beds with cream headboards stood in parallel. When I was four, Leng Dixon, the artist and illustrator my mother knew from Cape Town, and his wife, Phay, also an artist, came to stay, and they painted a full moon with a smile on my headboard and a sleeping crescent moon on the footboard. On Judd's headboard they painted a smiling resplendent sun with extending rays and a daybreak on the footboard. I had a temper tantrum at not getting the sun, to the embarrassment of Mom who ushered the Dixons quickly out of the bedroom. Ungrateful brat. The Dixons fascinated us children. We watched with sympathetic mouths open as they chewed every mouthful 32 times, making our mealtimes longer than patience would politely permit. A few years later we read in the news that social workers had taken away their two children for malnutrition. The mastication did not help much because Leng died at 52. One of his watercolours of the Malay Quarter hangs in my house – a late appreciation to recompense for my earlier unmannerliness.

My father's winnings at the track dictated any improvements or extensions of the house. A stone *braaivleis* built below the kitchen where we ate almost every Sunday evening. For a time, this tradition stopped because one Sunday, when the flames were already high, a squawk came from behind the burning wood from a bantam hen nesting on her eggs. The fire was too intense to reach her from in front and the built-in grid would not allow access from above, so she cooked while we spaded out the coals. For months, the braai area went unused. Thereafter we always checked before lighting the match. The swimming pool, built by the ever-busy Mr Harding, Builder, also sprang from a lucky bet, but lacked a filter pump. My father's only remedy was copper sulphate, so the water slowly turned green. This did not bother us. We played hide and seek because the "it" could not see through the pea soup. Neighbours, like Mike Simpson, did not like the idea of plunging into the murky liquid. My father bought a pump and the water from the pool was pumped out to water the garden, and, when empty, he filled it again and started the copper sulphate treatment. Winnings brought us built-in cupboards in our bedrooms and in the porch opposite the swimming pool.

Dad gambled on everything. He left office early on a Thursday to go to Turffontein racetrack. The wireless racing commentary on a Saturday afternoon percolated through the house. The rapid-fire delivery of the

St John on the top lawn of 17 Park St

commentator was astounding. I heard something like it again from the tobacco auctioneers in Salisbury. How did he know the names of the horses, follow the chronology of the race, repeat the names of the jockeys and the owners, know the colour of the jockey's shirt? My father followed the races with a well-annotated programme in his hand. When he bought a transistor radio, it followed him to the swing seat on the stoep and the radiogram in the sitting-room sighed with relief at not having to broadcast over the house. Judd, who worked with him after leaving school, said he bet on every shot on the golf course which meant that many club members at Parkview refused to join his fourballs. Judd said that Dad even received notes from bookies sympathising at his losses – unheard of from this cold- hearted and cynical class of skimmers. At the Durban July Handicap, he asked each of us if we wanted to place a bet and he took our money from us. In 1957, I asked him to place 10/-, two weeks pocket money, on *Migraine,* a malady I have suffered from all my life. He scoffed – it was a filly and fillies never won the Durban July. It came in at 16-1. He paid me £8, but I think my 10/- never went further than my father and the pay-out was from his own pocket.

The greatest compliment ever paid to my father came from Bill Coates, a massive, maverick Irish millionaire dairy owner who had unending admiration for my mother and who lived with the prima ballerina of the Cape Town Ballet, Dulcie Howes. He said, in wonder: "Eric never squeals". In other words, he always paid his losses uncomplainingly. Bill Coates joined the bridge foursome around our folding baize table where money of lesser amounts changed hands once a week. He gave us barbells and could lift two of us boys up by our belts above his head. It excited us to have Bill Coates arrive unexpectedly. Once his Dodge was parked in our drive. Who was here? He had gone next door to visit Rosemary Serrurier and then appeared around the swimming pool to the surprise of us all. He excited us because he did not speak to us but spoke with us quite unlike most of our parents' other friends. He said he kept a harpoon gun next to his bed: "I can reel the burglars in when I find 'em." At the house he had built himself in Benoni he had miscalculated the stairway to the first floor, so a visitor had to clamber on hands and knees up the last two steep steps to get upstairs. His garden was filled with American cars, a Cadillac, a Buick, a De Soto, a Chevrolet. He packed us boys into the back of one of them and drove us to the closest mine slimes dam in Germiston, surrounded by gum trees, the only tree to resist the harsh gold tailings and chemicals. Here he kept a Chris-Craft boat with two Evinrude 30 outboard motors. From this he towed an aquaplane. Judd was best at it and Bill Coates could ride fast with him, the boat aquaplaning over the yellowish water. The water was yellowish because the cyanide from the mine still stayed in the water. Falling in from the aquaplane meant your eyes stung and your skin itched.

One absentee from the circle of the Babbs was Joyce, Dad's elder sister. She had been alienated from my father for siding with the Peggy/Horace alliance. Amongst my father's papers I found a three-page letter written to Joyce in rhyme. He was a teenager at St John's and did not have anyone to visit on Sundays. The loneliness is palpable. All his teenage letters are achingly plaintive. He writes of the family being in Delagoa and of an outing where he shoots pigeons on a farm. Why was he boarding? Why did his father send him far away to Michaelhouse in Natal to matriculate? In 1933 he receives a certificate from a correspondence school giving him 96% for "salesmanship". To judge from the answers he typed to the questions, the school followed the Dale Carnegie method of persuasion. He writes essays and speeches for the "Q" Club on "The meaning of life" in which he quotes from Socrates and Greek legend. None of this learning is ever revealed to us children. He also did woodwork as a subject at school. That subject was reserved for the pupils who were not achieving academically. I have an oak desk he made at school. It is the one thing my eldest son wants from the inheritance.

We had one long meeting with Joyce when I was five, and then never again. My parents took Wayne and me in the Chev to stay with her for four days where she was living with her new husband near Witbank. This husband was a coalminer. He had bought a kraal, large and round and thatched. Joyce had had two children, Tim, a year younger than Wayne, and Hugh, eight months older than I. We all looked alike. We had the Babb features. This adventure of staying in a fairyland has etched itself into my mind which holds few other memories of my five-year old life.

The floor of the kraal was beaten mud. Each day a maid went on hands and knees and polished the floor with fresh cow dung. It did not smell but it polished up the floor to a sheen of extraordinary luminescence. Hugh and I stayed in the same room. Things were so new to me, so unexpected. There were fleas, a pest anyone who had animals and no DDT, endured. Hugh had a remedy for them – drop hot candlewax onto the bites and the itch dulled. The kraal did not have electricity, so candles were aplenty. Joyce sewed the clothes with a Singer sewing machine. She turned a handle on the wheel, manipulating the cloth under the needle's foot with the other hand. We awoke early to cock crow, something we knew in Joburg because we had bantams, but the first morning, as it grew light, the cow was lowing mournfully in the veld near the kraal. A calf was born in the night and lay, dead, behind the cow with the umbilical cord still hanging from under the cow's tail. Then another drama played out. The houseboy brought out a chicken, laid its head on a block and chopped it off. The squealing stopped but the two-legged creature did a death dance round the block, spurting blood. Joyce's husband took us into town and Wayne and Tim bought fishing flies. Logic told me that you could not catch a fish with the hook floating on the surface. I felt sorry that they had spent money on this useless apparatus. With string and long sticks, Wayne and Tim cast into the farm dam's muddy water and within ten minutes a carp had taken Tim's fly.

He also took us all to the Witbank flick house on Saturday morning. The programme consisted of short films like the Three Stooges but the *pièce de resistance* was the serial, continued every week and, to bring the punters back the next week, the serial ended at the most exciting part where the cowboy saw the rows of Indians on the edge of the hill above him. After the show, the kids gathered around to swap comics. We ate food cooked on an Aga stove. This was the region of the coalfields, after all, and the stove stayed heated all day, even warming the water for our baths in the zinc tub. "Can't I stay?" I said to Mom and Dad when they came to take us away from this wonderland. I never saw Joyce again, even at my mother's funeral, but Hugh and I are now like brothers and have met in Rome, Paris and Joburg. His numerous flock have also stayed with me – numerous because Gail, his wife, is Catholic. I met up with Tim who had emigrated as a vet to Manitoba, when I was ambassador in Ottawa. So, the next generation has kissed and made up. Hugh has promised to tell me more of the rift between Dad and Grandpop but has not yet. He stayed with Horace and Peggy often. "Horace used to swim every morning, just like you."

My mother's social aspirations were out of her reach. The closest she got to the Oppenheimers was being invited by Mrs Joan Pim, the Oppenheimers' landscape gardener, to tea at Brenthurst. The Oppenheimers lived at Brenthurst and the Oppenheimer domination of Joburg manifested itself in the Brenthurst Clinic, the Oppenheimer fountain and the Parktown Masonic Lodge on Louis Botha Avenue. What Mom did was to volunteer for charities. Her favourite was St Dunstan's for the Blind but that was not the only one that used her organisational skills. Helping charities was a social prerogative and duty. I was told by a psychologist that there is no such thing as altruism. The motive for any act of charity is also, or only, self-gratification. Mmm. He had a point, but some people have a generous nature with no sides to it. Mom's did not stint when she went into a campaign, but she also wanted the accolades that accompanied these sorties. Her scrap book has a plethora of photos and press articles of events she had organised. Before I started "real school", she was secretary of the African Feeding Scheme. One event was a visit to the Joburg zoo for black schoolchildren. I found the horde of several hundred uncontrolled and uncontrollable junior school kids scary, but the dozen tough biddies, nothing daunted, were distributing sandwiches, cake, cold drink and cookies to each of them. "Line up!" Mickey Stewart said. "Why do you want seconds, when you're still chewing the firsts?" Weenie Mauritzi berated a chubby eleven-year-old. "Pick up that wax paper! Don't leave the zoo in a mess," Winnie Campbell-Pitt scolded a delinquent boy, and he meekly did.

It was easier and more chic to raise the money with gala events rather than jumble sales and fêtes. My mother is photographed by newsmen with Pat Cowley at Drake's Drum music hall to fund the Southern African Youth Clubs, at a performance of the Royal Ballet with Sir John Maud, British High Commissioner and Joan Pim for the same charity, and, as acting chairman (*sic*) of St Dunstan's, with Mrs A Stamp (who had a daughter called Penny - honest) for another Drake's Drum. The idea of the Drake's Drum was inspired by Sir Francis, who, dying off the coast of Panama, called on his crew to take the drum that accompanied him in circumnavigating the world, to his home at Buckland Abbey and to beat it when England was in danger and he, Drake, would return to save his country. This seems a tenuous link to rescuing the poor, the blind, the crippled from disaster, but it had enough romantic pull for Mom to organise Drake's Drums. For the African Feeding Scheme, she arranged a ballet performance with the Cape Town Ballet and Dulcie Howes in the University Great Hall. Preceding this, some of the beneficiary tykes put on a stage performance. The play concerned a kraal, with a real rondawel on stage, catching the baboon who was eating their mealies. The actors put a calabash in front of the hut and disappeared behind the flats. An actor sneaked onto stage with a tail sewn to his brooks, looked left and right and plunged his hand/paw into the calabash and since his fist was balled, could not get it out again and sat and howled. The others appeared and, with cheerful joy, captured the baboon and led it off with a rope around its neck. Huge applause.

Less successful for St Dunstan's was a London evening. The man who fitted the London bobby uniform did not pitch up. The His Majesty's theatre was only half full. Weenie Mauritzi reluctantly clad me in the bobby's uniform. Then we went in to listen to Ann Ziegler and Webster Booth singing love songs from the thirties. The spare audience began tip-toeing out. They had had their snacks at interval. There was a small profit for St Dunstan's and Mom appeared again in *The Star* with me in the bobby uniform and honour was saved.

Her greatest success which elicits wonderment even today, was "The Appeal". At its diamond jubilee, St John's College sought to accumulate a building fund to extend the school to accommodate its growing number of pupils. The proposal was to have three nights of banquets and invite every Old Johannian to attend and to contribute to the fund. Mom managed to get herself voted that year as the chair of the Ladies Entertainment Committee of the school which arranged catering at school functions. This evinced jealous rage from Mrs Legg who was senior to Mom. From this elevated position, Mom choreographed a faultless three-day festival. It was a *tour de force* in which all her children were involved. Find the Old Johannians – no-one had a list or their addresses! Look names up in telephone directories and phone them. Ask them if they knew any of their classmates. Populate the list. Are you the person who matriculated in 1943 at St John's? "Write down the address properly, Glenn!" Hire a marquee. Hire linen, crockery, and cutlery. Check the menu and check again. Make sure there are washing

Charity Ladies – Mom, Joan Pim and Winnie Campbell-Pitt

up facilities. Bring in portaloos. The caterer who quoted the least was kosher, so all the utensils had to be "blessed by a priest or something, each time", my mother said. Print the invitations. Put stamps on the envelopes and send them. Keep an acceptance list. Order the wine. Arrange the tables and seating. Clear a field for parking.

A circus marquee stood for a week on the 'A' rugby field below the amphitheatre, all set up by Mrs Babb and the Ladies Entertainment Committee. Three times nine hundred guests came. Mom looked some of the guests up and down and said: "He never went to St John's. He's just taking a chance for a free dinner." Her zeal and attention to detail astonished everyone. Phyllis Callie, the mother of another three-son Johannian family wrote to Mom afterwards: "I stand amazed at all you have achieved and all with the greatest tact and good feeling. How lucky we were that your year of Chair coincided with the Appeal – truly, in our case, the Hour produced the Woman!" Deane Yates, the headmaster, was even more effusive: "I write to thank you for all you have done. It is an impossible task: I cannot adequately thank you … As we look back, we can see now how essentially vital the success of the dinners was: their success was the first, and fundamental essential of all our plans. This, dear Ora, is the sum of the debt we owe to you. Thank you for the wonderful effort you have made in carrying out the gigantic task that was allotted to you." The Appeal was the *summum nec plus ultra* of her mature life. What actually was the greater achievement, was Mom's detective work in seeking out Old Johannians and from that primitive list of addresses the school's precise record-keeping of alumni commenced. KC Lawson's book, *Venture of Faith,* records the triumph:

> "To accommodate nine hundred guests on three consecutive evenings was a staggering task; but Mrs Babb and her band of devoted helpers coped with it magnificently on 2nd, 3rd and 4th of September.
>
> "Nothing that could make the occasion a success was omitted: the decoration of the marquee with beautiful shields and floral arrangements; the splendid floodlighting of the College buildings

by a loyal Old Johannian; the supply and control of liquor; the provision of four thousand glasses for each night; the supply of water, electric light and cloak-room facilities; the co-ordination of the seating arrangements and reception by table hostesses; parking and traffic control – all were arranged with meticulous care down to the last detail; while the catering was of *cordon bleu* standard."

It was spoiled for her by what the school board did with the vast amount of money the Appeal gathered. Using the architects, Fleming's, who were the heirs to Sir Herbert Baker's firm which had designed the original buildings, the board was persuaded to go down the modernist path, even though Baker, as he always did with buildings and monuments he designed, had already drawn harmonious and corresponding extensions to the college on the ridge. The drawings were available to the architects, but they derided them. Deane Yates had been a marine in the forces and was not known for his taste. Presented with plans which only made passing reference to the Baker concept (such as a little dressed stone and small brickwork) and which gave "airy windows and strict straight lines" prominence, the board accepted this banal and unimaginative concept. Nobody liked the additions on the ridge. Artists and photographers who depict St John's buildings carefully exclude the new non-descript wing. Mom imagined a building reflecting the genius of Baker but got the workmanlike Joburg functionalism instead.

Mom liked the constancy of the rhythm of life. She was comfortable with a day that consisted of late breakfast served on a special breakfast tray on her bed. Of putting on the odd mudpack. Of a whisky and soda splashed from a syphon "when the sun has passed the yardarm". The Sparklet bombs became part of our array of toys and became real bombs in our games of war.

Then supper of three courses. As second son, I sat at Dad's left where the bread that Emily Nyati baked lay on the breadboard with a serrated knife. From the time I was promoted to the big table, I was the bread slicer. Each of us had our own napkin holder (napkin – serviette was non-U). It was at mealtimes that my mother gave me the worst advice ever: "Eat everything on your plate!" This was sometimes followed by the time-honoured: "Think of the starving Chinese." I still have difficulty in leaving food on a plate to the detriment of my waistline.

Under the carpet there was an electric bell push that Dad pressed with his foot at the end of each course. Knife and fork placed together, please, only crossed when you are still eating. Do not stack plates! Merlyn Sayers who stayed with us often, told me he was amazed that the houseman appeared precisely at the right time at the end of the course and had only learnt later of the bell. Then came coffee in small cups served in the sitting room. On Sunday, when there was no braai, carpet bowls or Monopoly. As we went to bed, Mom went into the pantry and unlocked the cupboards and carefully set out each servant's rations of sugar, tea and coffee. We were only excused Sunday lunch as an exception. Rare roast beef with Yorkshire pudding that Emily Nyati had learnt to cook at cooking school. Lunch never started before two on a Sunday because Dad spent a long time at the nineteenth hole at Parkview golf course. Since Sunday was an alternative off day for the servants, this tardiness irked the children, but Dad never returned earlier from golf.

The habitual, the known. You never needed to worry about a birthday or Christmas gift for my mother. She wore a gold charm bracelet from which hung gold stars, boats, small coins, Eiffel towers – an assortment which we examined with fascination and of whose origin Mom could tell you. Add to the collection. In the Christmas pudding one year, gold charms appeared. The tinkle of the charm bracelet gave comfort to the children as it moved round the house. Mom followed the Victorian pattern of affection. No hugging, no kissing. Boys shook hands. No arms around the shoulder. Pull up your socks. Boys don't cry. Take it on the chin. Stand on your own two feet. But even this distance can be taken as love. I only once saw my mother cry and I was so surprised I asked: "Why are you crying?" "Won't you cry when your mother dies?" I did.

The organisation of the household fell to Mom. On Tuesday, Neptune Cleaners with a swordfish painted on its panel van, came to collect the dry-cleaning and delivered it back on Friday. Two quarts of milk in glass bottles with hard cardboard stoppers arrived before daybreak from a Clover three-wheel bicycle deliveryman with a red clover painted on the icebox. The second most picturesque were the dustmen who gave loud, high-pitched whistles as they picked up the heavy zinc dustbins onto their shoulders, protected by thick leather shoulder pads to dump the contents into the slow-moving dustcart. Dogs barked continually as the whistling horde passed through the neighbourhood. The dustmen wore what had been left for them by property owners – shirts, blankets, sheets – round their waist. This category of employment was reserved to Zulus who would brook no other group from muscling into this domain. Georghiou's groceries arrived on a bicycle fitted with a huge, tapered wicker basket over its front wheel. We could have bought bread daily from Gallagher's Bakery in Orange Grove which sported round loaves painted on their Ford panel vans, looking rather like turds. Emily baked our bread. She had attended cooking lessons my mother arranged – bread, Yorkshire Pudding, Bread Pudding, stuffing for the chicken. As Gallagher's customers dwindled, the panel vans, all forlorn, stood broken and parked in the courtyard of the bakery and I longed badly to buy one and fix it. In winter, Wolpert's delivered coal. These deliverers were the most picturesque of all. The deliverymen, always jogging, bore a burlap sack, black with coaldust, over their heads, and their hands, clothes and heads were as black as soot, just the whites of their eyes staring wraith-like at us. They carried the fifty-pound sacks of coal on their shoulders and tipped the lumps into a coal-storage bin Dad had erected next to the garage.

Superstitions governed much of what she did. She even had a matchstick stuck into the upholstery of the blue Chev so she could touch wood when a hearse passed. Christmas decorations had to come down before twelfth night or the year would be unlucky. Black cats could pass in front but not behind. "See a pin and pick it up, all day long, you'll have good luck". 13 did not worry her but spilling salt did. "Take it with your right hand and throw it over your left shoulder into the devil's eye." Ladders – don't walk under them: practical advice. She said "touch wood" for anything she wanted to happen. "He'll be here at five, touch wood." "Break your bread before you butter it. In recognition of Jesus." Neither of my parents ever attended church or expressed any religious views but were very sniffy about Catholics and Jews. They insisted they were Anglicans. I made friends with a Catholic neighbour, Graham Brown, later to become an advocate. On Sundays I accompanied the family to the Roman Catholic Cathedral in Berea and sat in the car till mass was over. Graham bought a crucifix for his wall for 7/6. I asked Mom if she would give me 7/6 for a crucifix. Her horrified reaction surprised me. "Don't bring one of those into the house!" I had seldom seen her so troubled. The same visceral reaction came from Mrs Marike de Klerk when Pope John Paul gave her a rosary. She physically flinched and held it with the tip of her fingers. She could not wait to give it to my then wife. "*Hierdie dinge laat my gril!*" – these things make a shiver go up my spine.

She bought the school's 33 1/3 rpm record of Christmas Carols and my mother's favourite was the Russian Kontakion for the Departed. Another 33 1/3 she owned had Bach concertos and a rendition of "Jesu, Joy of Man's Desiring" she listened to at moments of nostalgia and sentimentalism. We were strictly forbidden to take the Lord's name in vain, but euphemisms for it passed our lips often: "Crikey!" "Blimey!" "Gosh!" "Bugger" and "bloody" held the record for the most used swearwords.

The bookcases were filled. Mom had two great penchants: Georgette Heyer, a mannerist novelist who researched the Regency period in fine detail and, according to critics, was precisely right about the minutiae of the habits and clothes of the time. The Berry books by Dornford Yates, suited her best. They are written by a barrister, Cecil Mercer, who gave up the bar after serving in the First World War and were best-sellers, though Alan Bennett, the writer, referred to Yates as "a practitioner of snobbery with violence, which runs like a good class tweed through the twentieth century literature". They provide a comic and nostalgic look at the leisured high-class society of the Edwardian era that gave Mom amusement. She could identify with that. They recount stories in large motorcars and events at the bar, where Mercer had encountered the seedier side of the London criminal and gang culture. The narrator is Boy Pleydell who comments on Bertram's (Berry's) doings. Mom bought them all: *Berry & Co, As Berry & I were saying, Berry Looks Back.* The author, Mercer, could not stand the English weather and after some years in Pau in France, he emigrated to Rhodesia where he served in the Second World War in the Royal Rhodesian Regiment and became a major. He died in Umtali in 1960.

Dad, in the American fashion, liked fat books (and thin women – his favourite was Esther Williams who, in each film, seemed to have a swimming scene). The blockbusters of Leon Uris, author of *Exodus*, James Michener author of *Hawaii*, and *The Source* the works of longer than 800 pages, took up lots of shelf space. We received a weekly literary boon. Mom received *The Saturday Evening Post* bearing the healthy and whimsical Norman Rockwell covers. For the boys, Mom turned to English comics. The weekly delivery arrived at Norwood Stationers and we begged Mom to take us to fetch them. *Radio Fun, Film Fun* and *Dandy*. You got absorbed into the characters the cartoonists depicted. Three favourites were Billy Bunter, "the fat owl of Greyfriars School" who represented six of the seven deadly sins – greed, gluttony, pride, envy, avarice and sloth, with a comical untruthfulness exemplified by his allusion to a non- existent postal order he was expecting from a "noble relation" to extract loans from his schoolfellows. Keyhole Kate peered, as her name suggested, through keyholes and knew secrets about all and sundry – in the later comics, she loses this waspish appeal by morphing into a Nancy Drew young, teenage detective. The last character was the obtuse but highly moral Desperate Dan who could burst through walls leaving a silhouette of his body in the bricks behind him. His jaw protruded beyond his chest and he shaved with a blowtorch. His favourite meal was cow pie out of whose crust two horns stuck. The authors of these strips were fully aware of the appeal of the foibles and the consistent comic nature of the storyline.

Both old folk were frugal. Dad frittered away a fortune on the horses, but we did nothing else extravagant. Money was always tight. The blue Chev, a Fleetline, and the grey Chev were the only cars in our car-pool. When I was still in Prep School and alone at home, a civil service looking man drove up the drive. He had slicked down Brylcreemed hair:

> "Brylcreem, a little dab'll do ya,
> Brylcreem, you're looking debonair,
> Brylcreem, the girls will pursue ya,
> Simply put a little in your hair".

Dismounting from the car, he asked me where my parents were. "Out", I replied suspiciously. He looked up at the house. "You'd better tell them," he said, looking at me with grim satisfaction, "that if they don't pay the bond, they'll lose the house." He got back into the car, turned it round and left down the drive with a thin trail of dust behind it. A cold shiver went through me. What was a bond? Why would we not keep our house? The cruelty of life became a reality. It paralysed me. I did not get comfort from the old man. I passed the message to him at the car door as he arrived. He just puffed crossly and said: "I'll sort it out" which was small comfort to me, and I panicked that he would not "sort it out". He did not know what terror lodged in my heart. Also cruel was a delivery by Georghiou's grocers after my mother's stroke. The bicycle with the load in the wicker basket arrived at the house and the deliverer said Andrew

Mom and Dad under the standard lamp where Mandy lay reading her books

Georghiou had said he could not deliver unless he was paid in cash. He handed the bill to Emily. Mom, in bed, said: "Tell him I don't have cash and I can't write a cheque because my right side is paralysed." This was not good enough for Andrew Georghiou and the deliveryman struggled back up the hill to Norwood with his full load. We never shopped at Georghiou's again. Perhaps our account had not been paid. My mother had helped Georghiou set up the grocery when he arrived from Cyprus, had done his books for him for free, she had got his grumpy father-in-law, Theo Kissernergis, to paint a watercolour of St John's College and bought the painting. She pointed out that the signwriter had misspelt "Delicatesen" on the overhang. I had taught his two boys English in hour-long sessions three times a week. No good deed goes unpunished. The Babbs had always had an account with Georghiou. We had accounts with everyone. From then on, Thrupps in Rosebank, which had an olive-green delivery panel van like Harrod's, brought the groceries and Mom opened an account there.

Mom did not ever work in gainful employment until after the Appeal. Mickey Stewart and she started an enterprise which flourished. It was called Rosebank Booking Service and had free office accommodation in Rosebank Hardware's shop. The service booked seats for any production or show in Joburg. By deft arrangements with the cinemas and theatres, phone bookings were accepted by the theatres and the tickets were picked up at the box office, taken to Rosebank and a commission was extracted from the theatregoer. It grew in popularity and even opened a booking office at the Stock Exchange. A further clever arrangement included the Greek café round the corner in Oxford Rd which provided a special despatch box to contain the envelopes and tickets which the client could pick up on the way to town where most of the theatres were. Both the hardware store and the Greek were glad of the extra traffic through their businesses. It grew so busy that Mom employed me one holiday to do counter duty. She sent me off to the Twentieth Century to queue for tickets for James Bond *Dr No*. These tickets were to be sold straight out of the Service. Through some misunderstanding I bought 200 tickets for each evening performance for a week, people behind me growing impatient and angry at my long sojourn in front of the box office. Mom was horrified. 1400 tickets! As they all sold quickly, she relaxed and at the end of the week I was back at the box office getting more.

Mom was now financially self-sufficient and even bought herself a Mini Minor, the chic car of the moment. So, too, was Mickey Stewart, who decided to retire from the business. She did what Horace had done to Dad: she left with all the funds and handed over signing power of the Booking Service. The work was exacting and time-consuming, clients even phoning our home for bookings. Then, as the computer age advanced, Percy Tucker, the impresario and theatre manager, who had competed with Rosebank Booking Service, began Computicket. The sale of tickets could be centralised and managed from a single point. Not all the theatres bought into the scheme which left lots of leeway for Mom, but once the theatres with their theatregoers moved to Computicket, Rosebank Booking Service had to wind down. The woman who ran the Stock Exchange office, who "was not one of us" ran off with the branch office funds and could not be traced. Clients had to be reimbursed and past-date tickets thrown away.

Andrew Georghiou's father-in-law Kissernergis' watercolour of St John's

Mom was no sportswoman but had a healthy regard for horses. Thank goodness for that. This is what gave Mandy an activity and a passion which was deep compensation for her through her youth. Mom did like animals. A bit too much. Stray dogs and the odd cat found their way into our menagerie. I picked up a mixed corgi-type dog which was wandering confusedly over Bryanston Drive through fast-moving traffic whom we called Mannfred. It was inoffensive and integrated well with other canine group until we discovered a name and telephone number on the rear side of its collar and we reluctantly returned it to its Bryanston owner. Despite the borzoi which stood next to Mom in her debutante photo, the animals we accumulated were curs of undistinguishable genealogy with exceptions like Piper of Redmayne, a dalmatian the Roseveares, who bred them, palmed off on her, against payment, I should imagine, because its spots were too far apart for a show dog. Well, sucks to the Roseveares. Judd took Piper to Kennel Club shows and won rosettes for first of breed and first of the show. One determinant remained – they had to be male and smooth-haired. We trusted dogs implicitly until, at six years old, I was sent to fetch Caroline Serrurier to come and play. On the way along their Catawba grape trellis arches, I patted the Serrurier's dog, a brute the size of an Alsatian called Boemie, its head at the height of my face. Without hesitation the mean cur grabbed my face in its jaws so that I still have scars on my right cheek and under my chin. I ran crying back home and have ever since been leery of others' dogs. Mom thought it enough to treat the two wounds with mercurochrome – none of this sissy anti tetanus jab. Someone else who underestimated tetanus was St John's College's house doctor, Dr Berry, whose son, Judgie, so close in name and looks to Judd, died of it after a banal wound at Pennington in Natal.

The cats had to "be snipped" or they sprayed over the furniture and carpets. Queen cats did enter the preserve and once, when I was eight, two litters of seven kittens were born at the same time. Mom hid this from Dad because she was a mistress at finding homes for kittens. Before they were weaned, they emerged all at once from their hideout in Judd's and my room and slipped, all of them, through the interleading door and marched in crocodile, tails happily in the air, into the sitting room (not the lounge, that was non-U). My mother sat there paralysed as this parade rounded the couch (not sofa that was non-U) and proudly proceeded over the carpet. One mewed and my father lowered one corner of *The Star*, saw this proliferation of life, folded the newspaper and went off to bed. Mom found homes for the kittens in record time.

She bought lights for the dogs from the butcher. An ungodly smell permeated the house when Emily cooked the heart, lungs, intestines and innards in a huge aluminium pot once a week. Emily cut the lights up and took a portion daily out of the Frigidaire fridge and descanted them out into the bowls next to the kitchen steps.

Bantams grew in numbers and were given away to Emily. We did not ask after their fate in Hammanskraal. They roosted in the four mulberry trees. Mom constantly unblocked the chicks' bottoms which clogged up with mulberry coloured poo. Guinea pigs did not last more than one generation when Mom saw that the male ate the offspring. Nor did the ducks. I thought it good to give Mom a duckling for Christmas. I bought it at a pet shop in town and the yellow, lively, orange-beaked unfledged bird was handed over to me in a brown paper bag. I carried this peep-peeping creature onto the Number 6 bus for Houghton and proudly presented it to Mom. A bit bemusedly she caged it behind chicken wire against the swimming-pool fence. This Heath Robinson affair did not constrain the duckling who was soon enjoying the waters of the pool. "It needs a mate", she said and soon two ducklings were flapping their flightless wings in the pool and counteracting any effect of the copper sulphate. The pool turned a duck-pond green. We could hide in that water if we played there. One of the two grew a little curl next to its tail – a drake. The three eggs hatched in the hutch near the pool. This joy was short-lived. On returning in the blue Chev one evening, the headlights fell on the corpse of the drake at the top of the drive and the duck was limping away in an awkward waddle from the bodies of her ducklings. The dogs of the neighbourhood had ganged up on them. Some madness had taken over their predatory instincts, even our own, who had cohabited peaceably with the ducks. The neighbours' dogs slunk away and ours, Pokey, Caesar and Piper, stood embarrassedly on the braaivleis lawn, guiltily wagging their tails. Mom gathered up the duck and dashed to the laundry where she desperately spooned iodine water into its beak and wiped mercurochrome on the wounds. It just looked sadly up at Mom. A tear fell from its eye as its neck flopped down. Tears sat momentarily in the corners of Mom's eyes.

Dad developed a hobby that lasted some years. He bought two beehives and put them on the garage roof. He also bought beekeeper's overalls, the cloth hood with gauze visor, long canvas gloves and the all-important smoker in which you put a piece of smouldering sacking. The smoker partially dazes the bees, so they are not aggressive to the person opening the hive. Dad had even invested in a divider which kept the larvae out of the combs. He successfully gathered, in square wooden frames with wire netting, combs with rich honey. He decided one Sunday after lunch to harvest honey. I was eight, Judd six and Wayne on the brink of teenagehood. It was late in the afternoon. Dad had spent more time than usual at the nineteenth hole and was mellow after the Sunday roast. A summer storm was brewing. Dark clouds were gathering on the Southern horizon. The pre-storm wind was picking up. Dad only put on his gloves and the hood without the overalls and started the smoker, squeezing on the handle of the blower to keep it going. He climbed up our short ladder and stood near the hives. The bees were becoming very agitated both by the coming storm and the human presence. They were buzzing angrily around Dad. He pumped on the smoker. It had gone out. The bees intensified their buzzing. They gathered closer around Dad who has now swatting at them desperately with both arms and gloves. Mom gathered the children up and jogged for the porch door. Dad was now banging his arms against the hood and trying to find the top of the ladder with his foot. The swirling multitude about him had grown immense so you could hardly see him through the swarm. The angry hum grew deafening and frightening. Mom shut the porch door behind her. We turned around but could no longer see the dramatic scene but could hear the vicious anger and the deep vibration of the mass of furious wings. A few seconds later Dad rushed at the door, a globe of bees swishing around him and banged for admission. Bees hit the glass with force and hard pings. Mom would not let him in. In desperation he turned round, still waving his arms and hitting his head, towards the swimming pool. He had to leap over the gate. But he stopped at the edge? Jump, Dad! No, he was taking off his suede shoes.

The whole swarm followed him onto the surface of the water and there was an eerie silence as the brown, teeming mass spread out over the whole pool, wriggling and struggling. Dad stayed under water a while. When he came up and took a breath, his hood now off, bees stung him in the mouth. A few stragglers still circled the pool. He got out of the pool with bees' bodies spattered over his clothes and Mom let the sodden victim into the house. He took off his clothes in the green bathroom and went to bed. Dr Bovet came to give him an adrenaline injection. He stayed in bed two days. I had never seen my father in bed during the day. We went, when we were allowed next morning, to look at the pool, still covered with a carpet of bees. Next to the side were Dad's suedes. A veil of beestings covered each shoe. They stuck out in T's from every bit of soft leather.

Dr Bovet was the society doctor of Joburg. The northern suburbs had deep respect for him – after all, he was Swiss. He did house calls and had a practice on the first floor of the Dunvegan Chambers opposite the Witwatersrand Supreme Court building and kitty-corner to John Orr's department store. He treated us when we got measles, chicken pox and mumps. Twice I visited his rooms. Once when I was little with my mother at Daggie Lenning's, I had been unable to pee. My foreskin had stuck to the glans. So much for bathing every night. With a bit of cream, he loosened it from the knob. When I was reaching teenagehood, Mom took me to see him about my migraines. No-one in the world understood migraines then. Bovet had information that migraines could be linked to diet. "Don't eat fat and sweet things," he said in his Frenchified accent. He was right about triggers, but not those. No child could avoid fat in the Babb household, but I did discover that Coca Cola was such a trigger and I have never drunk it since.

Two acres of garden need a strong gardener. Ours was Johannes Ramagalies. One of his sayings entered the household vocabulary. Juddy pottered around the area where Johannes was planting, taking seedlings away or picking up rocks from the edge of the bed. Johannes was a man of few words; he shouted at Juddy: "I'll smack you before I cry you", which was a perfectly logical threat and was used by all of us after that. Johannes was enormously strong. When Mom was building a fishpond to replace the paddling pool, Johannes carried a 100lb rock on his right shoulder and dumped it at the pond's edge. This became the feature of the pond, a place of reverie and wonder. Look at the spawn on the surface. Look how the tadpoles wiggle their tails and cling to the wall. Listen to the plop of the frogs jumping in. The willow Mom, or rather, Johannes, planted above it grew and prospered and we swung on its branches over the pond. Masked weavers wove their intricate nests in the branches. It was *Salix sepulcralis*, a weeping willow. None of us knew that willows are male and female and their catkins on separate plants are of different sex. It went unpaired. The pond was at the top of the bottom lawn that stretched down to the road. Johannes mowed this expanse with a small hand mower.

Johannes had a passbook with pages to tear out on perforations. Mom would tear one out and write in her permission for absence from his place of work. This meant he could go anywhere without facing arrest or harassment, but it also meant that he could visit the shebeens which was the purpose for his absence. Beer. Kaffir beer, it was called then. Emily Nyati was a champion beer brewer. This is a primary task of the woman in a tribe and a good brewer was a desirable wife. A stream of visitors to Emily's room was a daily and tolerated phenomenon.

Mom, ever attentive to the folk around her, let the teams of weeding ladies who knocked on the door scatter out over the lawn and pull out the weeds. She gave them weeding tools and they set to work, sitting on blankets, breast-feeding their infants from time to time and desultorily making a pile of weeds. They were not good at getting the roots out, but Mom paid them anyway. She grumbled afterwards but when the team came back, she again let them spread out over the lawn. She badly wanted a picket fence at the road but right until we sold part of the property to the Tepersons, the boundary to Park Street remained a slack wire held up by three short fence poles. No use putting up a name board, "Meadowbanks" once the lawn was gone.

Johannes had a "cousin", a sophisticate who arrived in jacket and tie on a bicycle with a basket over the front wheel. In the basket, he transported seedlings, each in soil carefully wrapped with thick brown paper and tied up with brown, rough string. He had a little watering-can to keep the seedlings damp. He never went away without Mom buying something. Her pride was the rose garden. Judd and I were allotted a plot there to plant and were given seeds. My plot lay under the lemon tree, Judd's against the Goldberg's wall. Judd lost interest and nothing grew – a foretaste of his gardening at St John's College where he was also allotted a plot to plant. This was good camouflage for him and David Potter to quietly go and have a smoke at break. The rose garden was the only formal part of the garden. Each rose stem grew in its own circular bed and provided roses for the house throughout the summer. In the Witwatersrand winter, all was bleached dry, the lawns became beige, the pond froze over and Johannes spent his time sweeping.

In the lower part of the garden under the acacia trees, Johannes had dug a compost pit. Into this pit all vegetable matter was dumped. Including the grass clippings. After rain, the grass clippings floated to the top of the now water-logged pit. We three brothers convinced friends who visited to walk over the carpet of grass clippings, and although suspicious, they gingerly tiptoed over the grass and found themselves waist-deep in compost water. Mom could never convince us to stop this trick which resulted in providing dry clothes to the visitors. You could tell that she was inwardly amused.

My parents' world turned topsy-turvy when the Nats came to power in 1948. They had always been Smuts followers, but Jan Smuts in his dotage had, like Nelson Mandela later, become obnubilated by the international adulation he enjoyed. My autograph book has a signature by Jan Smuts signed on a Johannesburg Chamber of Commerce dinner menu – so you can say that they had at least met him. He advanced the 1948 election so that he could fit in his visit to Cambridge to be the first foreigner ever to be inaugurated as Chancellor of the University. This was far more important to him than the paltry politics of South Africa. He lost the election just as Churchill, his devoted acolyte, did. The Nats moved quickly and legislation restricting movement, residence and employment of Blacks rapidly passed the parliamentary test despite the best efforts of the Torch Commando and Smuts' United Party.

Johannes Ramagalies with his flexible passbook (called "reference books" in Orwellian newspeak just as the Nats later called the Bantu Affairs Department "Plural Relations" - What is a Bushman painting? "A rural plural mural") let him wander where he may. Philemon, who always wore a suit and a trilby hat, escaped the cops' street checks because of his smart appearance.

The election of 1948, despite what the analysts say, had far less to do with black-white relations. It fundamentally reflected the historic animosity between the English-speakers and the Afrikaners. It was revenge for the Boer War. Mom would sniffily refer to the guerrilla tactics of the Boers as "unfair and ungentlemanly". Now the Afrikaners had the heft in the hand. The first worry for my mother was how the education policy, enforcing separate schools for Afrikaners, would affect her friends. She worried that the boys at St John's with Afrikaans names, the Joostes, the Baerveldts, the du Plessis would be forced to leave the school and go to Afrikaans schools. The Nats prioritised the armed forces, the judiciary and education to boost Afrikaner control. My parents were incensed that war heroes were demoted or pensioned off and replaced with Afrikaners who had not fought in the Second World War in which, proportionately, more Afrikaners had enlisted than English-speakers.

The Nats, many of whom had been interned during the war, including the future Prime Minister, BJ Vorster, and the head of the intelligence service, "Lang Hendrik" van den Bergh, did not trust the English-speakers or their loyalty to South Africa. Not until twenty years later were English-speakers appointed to the Cabinet in the form of Frank Waring and Alfred Trollip. The distrust was mutual. The grandfather of one of my best friends, Piet Lloyd, owned a plot North-East of Johannesburg. He had pigs and the first two born after the election, he called Dr and Mrs Malan – the name of the Nat Prime Minister.

My secretary in Paris, whose name was Phyllis Liebenberg, recounted how boys threw stones at her on the way back from school during the war because her surname was Liebenberg, which the local English-speakers took to be German.

How did my parents react? Firstly, they gave up cigarettes from Anton Rupert's Rembrandt company, which they did not smoke anyway. On their deaths a whole box-load of smoking equipment appeared: silver lighters, silver ashtrays, cigarette holders, silver cigarette cases, silver cigarette boxes. They were powerless to show their fury. They lived in a constituency, Houghton, which was a safe United Party seat. They worried when the South African Police built a large barracks to house policemen in the constituency specifically to increase Nat voter numbers in Houghton. No chance. It was Helen Suzman's constituency even when she left the United Party. It could not be prised from the opposition's hands, even though the United Party put up a candidate, General Steyn, to oppose Helen Suzman. She often visited our house at election time and my parents became Progressive Party supporters. I was more sanguine about her. Claude Charbonnel was a bridge partner with her and recalls a conversation at one of the bridge drives when salaries for domestics came up: Claude reported her as saying: "No more than seventy-five rands a month." When Tony Leon got himself made candidate in the place of Irene Mennell, Helen Suzman's preferred successor, she said it was "manipulation worse than Tammany Hall", the most corrupt Democrat district in New York. Anyway, when I went to see her before leaving for Canada as ambassador, she gave me some of the best advice I have ever received: "Don't try and justify the unjustifiable."

The 1948 election galvanised the ex-servicemen and the *Sappe*. It was a touch-and-go affair. Smuts had refrained from redrawing the constituency borders, so rural constituencies had a weighted advantage dating from the time when rural constituencies presented farmer candidates. After the elections, graffiti appeared everywhere of a large 'V' which contained a question mark. This implied the election was not the *Volkswil* -People's Will – because, in total, far more had voted for the United Party than for the Nats. Even though a greater proportion of Afrikaners had enlisted for the war, the returning servicemen were not given their due in housing and education, so many had turned against Smuts and the United Party – except what the Afrikaners called the *Bloedsappe* – the dyed-in-the-wool United Party supporters in the *platteland*. Feverish activity gripped the United Party organisers – hardly worth it in such a safe seat as Houghton, but I sat on Mom's lap as she sealed party manifestos into envelopes at the United Party's organiser's house in Pretoria Street where dozens of women stuck on stamps and phoned voters. It was frenetic but hopeless because the Nats won the general election with the help of the Afrikaner Party of Nicolaas Havenga, who had also opposed South Africa' entry into the Second World War.

Mom was infuriated when the Nats pardoned and released Robey Leibbrandt, imprisoned for treason after Smuts had revoked his death sentence. Leibbrandt was an Olympic bronze medal boxer at the Berlin Olympic Games in 1936 and was enraptured by the Nazi Party. He became South African heavyweight champion in 1937 and went back to Berlin for training at the athletes' Reich Academy for Gymnasts and stayed on after war broke out, enlisting in the *Wehrmacht*. The Germans trained him as a glider pilot and he attended a special unit for irregular warfare, called *Quenzgut*. At the end of the sabotage training, he was inducted into *Operation Weissdorn* (Operation Hawthorn) whose aim was to engineer a *coup d'état* against the Smuts government. He landed in June 1941 from a French sailboat off the Namaqualand coast and worked his way to the Afrikaans anti-war organisation, the *Ossewabrandwag* (The Ox-wagon Sentry). The leader of the OB, as it was called, Dr Johan van Rensburg, was little impressed by Leibbrandt who defected with 60 OB supporters to start a campaign of sabotage, dynamiting electricity pylons and railway lines and cutting telephone and telegraph lines. In December 1942 he was recognised during a skirmish with Union Government troops and was captured. He refused to participate in his trial at which he gave the Nazi salute and said he acted for *Volk und Fuhrer*. When sentenced to death, he shouted: "I welcome death!" to applause from his supporters in the public gallery.

Somehow, in my autograph book, there is a signature of Robey Leibbrandt. Underneath, Mom has drawn a firing squad with multiple bullets hitting a blindfolded Leibbrandt.

One of the Nats' economic revival policies after the war involved import substitution – a disaster for HE Babb & Son because import of lots of consumer products was subject to import control and HE Babb & Son only had agencies for imported goods. A permit was needed for all imports of listed items. An easy target presented itself in the clothing and fabrics business. The government set up state-owned enterprises and for the wool industry it was called Wolnit. The chairman of this quango was an academic who had never been in business or manufacturing, a Dr Visser. I even tried out my prep school Afrikaans on him when he phoned in the evenings and he phoned often. Dad was made member of the board because he sat on the Chamber of Commerce's import committee and was asked to co-operate in getting those manufacturers that HE Babb & Son represented to set up joint ventures in South Africa. Mom despised Dr Visser. "He spits when he talks. He speaks only Afrikaans in his speeches". Wolnit was big on dinners and promotions and small on enterprise and manufacture. With academics in charge, Wolnit came, after two years, to an ignominious end. It now does not even merit a mention on the internet.

When Judd joined HE Babb & Son, he quickly saw that this import control system had flaws and soon he was getting clients to swap and sell import permits and he navigated round the restrictions in a way my Dad would never have imagined. Dad was furious when Judd phoned Cannon Towels in the USA about a tender for a large quantity of towels – a phone call is expensive: telegraph. He was appeased when HE Babb & Son won the tender. The telegraph: the cost was per word – 2d. But you had to spell out the punctuation. "HAVE REACHED HERMANUS STOP. STEMIGLENN", all in capitals. The last word was a mixture of Steve, Michael, Glenn – the three who had gone adventuring together, but the Post Office clerk would not accept it as one word, so we had to pay 4d. more. One jokey mock-up I read went: "IM COMING STOP NO DONT STOP PLEASE STOP NO DONT STOP YES STOP".

By the time Judd entered HE Babb & Son, my Dad was coasting on the established clients that gave him the turnover needed to keep going and keep gambling – the men's shops and department stores ensured orders even as import control intensified. Markhams, Manhattans, where Dad spent a lot of time chatting and taking tea, McCullough and Bothwell, all self- standing shops with their own comfortable buildings in the city centre, and the department stores John Orr's, Stuttafords, Ansteys, Cuthberts. Judd was impatient with this dull carousel and got the agency for Lee Jeans and started a cut-make-and-trim business for BVD with his friend, John Piguet.

Joburg radiates out from the city centre. Buses started at the central bus terminus at the end of Eloff Street in Marshalltown. Eloff Street was the *nec plus ultra* for a posh and expensive business address. A common expression used by Joburgers to show disbelief was to say: "If that's true, I'll buy you a farm in Eloff Street." To get from one suburb to another, the commuter had to travel to central Joburg and take the bus from there to reach his next destination. Dad only used the grey Chev, stopping daily at the Jeppe Street Post Office to pick up the mail in PO Box 1255 and re-join Philemon in Twist Street to drive to the one-way von Brandis Street where Philemon found a parking space for the day until the Council introduced parking meters. Then Dad hired monthly parking at the Pritchard Street garage. The garage was a modern Swiss wonder of the time. Cars were lifted automatically to their place. When the machinery broke down irreparably, the lack of ramps meant that the cars parked there were permanently stuck on their floor. The grey Chev was not amongst them.

The centre of town was the place, *the* place. Everything of importance took place in town. The best restaurants attracted their customers to town: for sophisticates, *Chez André* in Kruis Street, The Criterion in the Carlton Hotel, The Blue Grotto in the Colosseum Building and, of course, His Majesty's Grill. Dad's watering hole lay straight over the road from his office, Dawson's Hotel, which provided the simple English fare he preferred, though his favourite cheese was *Bel Paese*. He only once invited me to lunch with him at Dawson's and, at seventeen, I drank my first glass of wine, a Nederburg Stein. Lady Ann Barnard writes in her diary about Stein wines in 1797:

"Lord bless me, what fine wine this is!" said he; "I have not tasted a glass such as this since I came here!" I then found, on asking, that it was Steine wine, a cheap Cape wine, which Mr Barnard had not liked and had ordered for common use in the household."

Eric Babb Chairman of the British Manufacturers' Association

The old man favoured beer and whisky. His tastes were pedestrian and lacking in pretension. He was a member of the Union Club in town, a laddish place of beer and skittles. He eschewed the preciousness of the Rand Club, the summit of all meeting places for the Joburg élite which had a separate entrance for ladies. Downstairs in the Rand Club were the superb marble loos with shiny brass taps and black and white tile floor and a uniformed attendant to hand over hand towels and polish the taps with Brasso. Dad took me to the Union Club only once to have a sandwich at the bar and to play snooker at which he was quite accomplished and me, not so much. To see the cues' tips being rubbed with blue chalk, the rack for the cues, the wooden scoreboard with brass pointers and the long extension rests was a thing of wonder. A good snooker player is the sign of a misspent youth. The ritual around the baize- topped slate table and rounded teak legs has its own mystique and rhythm which was only spoiled for me by Jodie Foster's film, *The Accused*, in which the victim is gang-raped on a pool table. I was no good at snooker, but I did not slice open the baize.

One of the three annual outings Mom arranged for the family took place in town: the pantomime. This took place at the Colosseum, the star-spangled and elaborate art déco cinema Liberty Life razed to the ground, shame on them. The first time Wayne went to the pantomime, I was too little. On the arrival of the Widow Twanky on stage, Wayne crept under the folding seat and did not emerge until she was offstage. Boswell's Circus erected its tent on open ground next to the Rand Showgrounds in Braamfontein. Boswell's was trad in every way: sawdust spread over the ring, ringmasters putting their heads in the lions' jaws, elephants standing on hind legs on a tub, girls in tutus riding standing on horses' backs, trapezes, human cannons and Tickey the Clown. Boswell's, later Boswell Wilkie's, repeated the dose every year. Each year we were in terror of the lions' incisor going through the ringmaster's skull, gnawing our nails at the trapeze artists, waiting for the spray of shredded paper from Tickey's bucket to reach the front rows of the ring. It might have been always the same, but we were absorbed by it, went to the cages afterwards to see the lions and elephants and watched in awe the spangled ladies returning to their caravans. Never once did we think of the agonising training all these animals went through to entertain us. Giving something too much thought takes out the mystery and the illusion. Perhaps a word about the monstrosity of subjecting animals to all that would have given us pause, but I treasure the innocent enthralment we could enjoy.

Every century has its mode of expressing itself: the play and the theatre in the 17th century, the symphony and orchestras in the 18th, the novel in the 19th, but the film, unlike any other magical influence, provided the universal primary expression of the 20th. Joburg even boasted a 20th Century Fox cinema. The places for the film were bioscopes, though Mom insisted that we eschew that South Africanism and only use cinema. The films themselves were not the subject of Mom's censorship. No, it was the place where we might meet rough people that she disapproved of. Flick houses in the Southern suburbs were out of bounds. At a pinch, we could go to the Gem in Kensington, the Victoria on Louis Botha Avenue in Orange Grove and the Piccadilly in Yeoville, the suburb of Sol Kerzner. The matinée was the place for teenage encounters. A prized possession shown off at school was a comic book imprinted with lipstick off the lips of your date.

Central town was not out of bounds for flicks and for the mesmerising attraction of movies, Joburg had a cluster of flick houses. The Plaza in Sauer Street showed all the Elvis Presley films. This attracted the Braamies Boys, bikers who drove fear into the hearts of the good burghers of Joburg. They typified the rough crowd. I saw them as they emerged from 6 o'clock show at the Plaza. Their bikes were parked in cohorts along both pavements of Sauer Street, Harley Davidsons, Nortons, BSAs, Royal Enfields and Triumphs. They called them "irons". No Japanese bikes. Those they called "plastics". Nobody who owned a plastic entered the Braamies Boys. The leader came from Braamfontein which lay straight up Sauer Street over Queen Elizabeth Bridge a mile away. Out of the Plaza the Braamies

Boys streamed. They wore their Brylcreemed hair swept back and combed behind in an upward coiffe. Like a drake's tail. The Braamies Boys were the quintessential ducktails, rebellious and violent. Most had a cherry with them all wearing the stiff 32-foot petticoat then in vogue. The chicks pushed the stiff taffeta net down between their thighs and mounted the motorbike pillions behind their leather-jacketed escorts and hugged them round their waists, the net petticoats spread out on both sides. The Braamies Boys kick-started their machines and an unholy roar filled the air as they revved. Some of the bystanders blocked their ears. They lined up at the corner of Sauer and Commissioner Streets, three hundred of them. The Joburg traffic cops wearing their shiny calf-length boots and crash helmets marshalled them and cautiously shepherded them into place stopping other traffic. The leader, bearing a German imperial helmet with spike, stood on his footrests, looked back at his cohorts, waved his arm in a circular motion and the cavalcade growled up the hill toward Braamfontein with the traffic cops warily in their wake, alert to any misdeeds, except passing through red robots. Back at the Plaza, the watching crowd began to disperse except for a few who were sniggering as a Braamie, cherry on the pillion, tried desperately to kickstart his machine, only managing to get a sad brrrm! brrrm! sound as the cylinders revolved lifelessly.

We could get permission to go to movies at the Bijou in Jeppe Street which, long after the other flick houses, programmed a long entrée to the feature film. This included singing to the bouncing ball. The projectionist projected the words onto the screen and a white ball hovered over each of the words of the song as it was sung, a sort of group karaoke: "How much is that doggie in the window" – long pause of the ball over "dog-", short jumps on "-gie in the window". The music caused herd enchantment. It came from a huge Wurlitzer organ which rose from the orchestra pit as the words appeared. Dean Herrick made his name playing at the Bijou. He played for the South African Broadcasting Corporation. He played for the Symphony Orchestra. He played at important ceremonies, but the Wurlitzer stayed at the Bijou until the public tired of it. Mom said the ladies went to matinées at the Bijou to see Dean Herrick's organ rise.

His son, also Dean, still owns the organ, but the Bijou and its bouncing ball is long gone.

The Colosseum in Commissioner Street was the monster art déco movie house which doubled also as stage for major live shows. Here we saw the pantomimes, here I saw Ray Charles playing the ivories, here I attended the only rock concert I have been to. It was Cliff Richard and the Shadows. The girls in their stiff petticoats stood through the whole show on the velvet seats of the Colosseum, screaming without let-up: "Hank! Hank!", the name of the lead guitarist, Hank Marvin. You could not hear the music above their high-pitched screams. The teenagers wanted Hank, Cliff Richard less so. A stadium manager told me that the clean-up after a rock concert included washing the fabric on seats with vinegar. He did this because the teenyboppers wet themselves when their idols appeared. The *Sunday Times* reported on its front page how, in front of the City Hall, Cliff had kissed a fan for 11 seconds. So unrewarding was the rock concert experience that I never went to such a concert again.

I did go to the flicks at the Colosseum with Shirley Campbell, dressed impeccably and wearing her hair in lacquered waves. I had fetched her from the hairdresser in Hillbrow where I had my first and only street fight. Judd and David Potter were with me and while we walked on the sidewalk some ducktail whistled at Shirley. I was so proud to be with her that I turned on the oaf and landed a first blow, but he shoved me against the show window of a Portuguese market gardener and sneered: "I know Ju-Jitsu" and stalked off. At the Colosseum, the boy in the seat next to her was playing with his gas lighter making the flame shoot higher and higher till it caught Shirley's lacquered hair and a minor conflagration started on her head which I quickly put out. The boy apologised profusely, but he was the one I should have landed the blow on.

His Majesty's Theatre presented plays and musicals like "Annie Get Your Gun". I was incensed that Annie Oakley deliberately loses the shooting match to submit to Frank's ego. The songs like "You cain't get a man with a gun" and "I've got the sun in the mornin' and the moon at night" keep on turning in my head and determined my later musical proletarianism.

In the same street as HE Babb & Son, von Brandis, Twentieth Century Fox built a red brick monstrosity with the clearest architectural no-no, a blank wall four storeys high across which featured a huge metal "20" stretched from edge to edge and on the other side of the corner site. This was the home of the blockbuster movies, James Bond, "My Fair Lady", "Poseidon Adventure". The Metro and the Empire fulfilled the same function. Schlesinger's son, John, sold his whole empire of African Consolidated Theatres to 20th Century Fox which took over all of Schlesinger's cinemas.

This left the art house cinemas to show British and dubbed French films. The Pigalle was in the city centre but the Piccadilly was in Yeoville, close enough to St John's College for us pupils to walk in crocodile to watch the documentary on Queen Elizabeth II's coronation in 1953. Mom dropped me off to see "The Magnificent Seven", but its Japanese inspiration, "Seven Samurai", I saw at the Pigalle with subtitles.

There were still gaps in the market to skirt the Schlesinger monopoly which depended on the Hollywood flicks. So, around Johannesburg, drive-in theatres sprang up in the 50s in emulation of the Americans. Until we were eighteen and licensed to drive, we had to implore our parents to take us to these new phenomena – the Top Star, installed on the top of a goldmine dump overlooking Joburg, the Velskoen in Randburg and the Pretoria on the road to Pretoria. Those with station wagons reversed on to their little hump so that the whole family could lie in the back, but where did you put the speaker from the pole? It had to hook onto the back window, and if you could not hear it, the soundtrack came from all the cars around you. To pep up the flick experience, the Cinerama opened with a wrap-around screen to give the impression to the audience of being part of the action. The Cinerama also was the first to start 3-D movies. It was a badge of pride to show off to your friends the cardboard spectacles holding the bi-coloured cellophane lenses.

Mom preferred us to go to the six o'clock show because then she could pick us up at a reasonable hour, but if the bus timetable allowed for a ride back at the end of the flick, we could come home on the No 6 (Abbotsford) or the No 10 (Norwood) bus.

Films came to South Africa two months after their showing in Europe or America. Isidore W. Schlesinger and his son, John, had an excellent relationship with the newspapers' critics who wrote up the new releases long before they came to our screens. We had two months of anticipation and excitement before the opening nights. Queues formed outside the box offices. Getting seats was a lottery without prior booking until Rosebank Booking Service could do the queuing for the public. You needed to see the film the first time round because you would not get the chance again. Some of the outlier movie houses did bring back classics. Because the parents of Graham Brown invited me, Mom allowed me to see "African Queen", at the Gem in Kensington. It was a disappointment because Katherine Hepburn had immaculate make-up throughout even on the Congo River. I later bought the house opposite the Gem on Roberts Avenue and then sold it to the owner of the Gem.

The pattern of movie-going, until Ster-Kinekor took over the business, repeated itself as dictated by Isidore Schlesinger, Killarney Studios and African Consolidated Theatres. It was invariable: trailers for upcoming movies, African Mirror news, the news shorts whose content changed according to local developments (and whose past reels Killarney Studios criminally burnt on the pyre in front of the studios), a cartoon, Looney Tunes or Disney; Tom & Jerry with its inherent violence had the audience shouting and clapping. Then came interval. Big popcorn machines spluttering behind the glass screen. Cream soda. Milk shakes at the counter. Chappies chewing gum, wrapped with striped paper on whose reverse three jokes were printed. Woe betide you if the third punchline couldn't be fitted on to the little sheet. Chewed gum stuck under the flick house chairs. Mom denied us permission to go to the café- bios. The old movies showed there and moviegoers ate their lunch and drank their beer watching the movie from counters at which they were served. Rough people there. I snuck in during the hols when I was a teenager. The doorman and the box office clerk did not care that I did not look eighteen. The film's dialogue was hard to hear because of the clanking of cutlery and china.

All this mystique and enchantment faded with the arrival of television. Ster-Kinekor had bought out 20th Century Fox in 1969 in a diminishing market, compounded later by television's arrival. The magical theatres were replaced with multiplexes with smaller movie houses in shopping centres in appalling taste with carpets crawling up the wall, automatically run projectors and wrap-around sound. When our embassy moved to Quai d'Orsay in Paris in 1974, the architect covered the ambassador's office with purple carpeting stretching right up to the ceiling. The South African staff called it the Ster-Kinekor room.

After picking us up from the early show, Mom and Dad took us to the Doll's House. One was in Berea near the General Hospital but attracted people "who were not like us" so the preferred venue was inevitably the Doll's House in Orange Grove on Louis Botha Avenue. On a large, macadamised parking lot stood proudly a quadrangular building with a steep, red-tiled roof with dormer windows, white brick work and shutters at all five windows. Yes, it did look like a doll's house. Clients parked as close to the building as possible. Over the stoep roof the legend "Flick Lights for Service" appeared, which did not help in daylight, followed by the admonition "Do Not Hoot!" From this brick house came marvellous toasted chicken and mayonnaise sandwiches, milk shakes – even orange milk shakes – chicken in the basket, chips, toasted tomato and cheese sandwiches, tubs of ice cream. On Saturday after ten, do not expect to find a spot for your car. The cars were parked so close to each other that the waiters and waitresses had difficulty holding the tray above their heads as they crabbed their way between them. Under each tray was welded a contraption that hung the tray on your half-opened window and supported itself against the door with a rubber-ended arm. Rubber-ended so it did not scratch your precious Pontiac paintwork.

Mom and Dad attended live theatre at the Brian Brooke Theatre and the Playhouse. Mom took us to see "The Boyfriend" and bought the long-playing record which she almost wore through listening to "Won't you Charleston with me?" and "It's Never too late to Fall in Love". More serious plays made her bite her nails. George Bernard Shaw's "St Joan" and "The Gazebo", a play about a blackmailed couple. This was made more accessible because Rosebank Booking Service sometimes got complimentary tickets

The rainy season came to an end at the Rand Easter Show. The inevitability of at least one rainstorm coinciding with the Show was taken for granted. Mom made all the children members of the Witwatersrand Agricultural Society which organised the Rand Show. By the time we attended, the only agricultural part of the show surviving was the cattle competition. The breeds passed in review in the show-jumping ring. Here stern men wearing suits and homburgs handed out the rosettes that hung thereafter in the bulls' stalls. The Society issued enamel badges on golden chains and bars for the lapel. In the middle of the badge stood the year of issue. This gave you free entry to the show and entrance via a side gate where you avoided the queue. This was not the reason for our membership. It was the loos. Mom did not want us to go to the public ablutions. The Clubhouse had clean lavatories.

It also gave us free access to the show-jumping at the arena in front of the Clubhouse and this is what Mom most wanted to attend. Watching the jumping became more and more attractive. I especially liked the Portuguese military competitors from Mozambique in grey uniforms and bedecked with a military headwear rather than the black velvet helmets with a spliced ribbon hanging out of the back the others wore. White jodhpurs and hunting jackets in scarlet or black. The water jump, the triple-jump and the hedge. It seemed unfair that merely tipping over a bar with a hind hoof meant losing a point. Six-year-old riders controlling a ton of horse. Mom, who had ridden in Cape Town, came to watch all the finals and cheer the clear rounds. But the horsemen and horsewomen belonged to a different breed to us. I stood at the fence and watched. Marie Burbach, sister of my friend Gilbert, walked her horse along the fence and handed me an empty Coke bottle. With a gesture of her hand, I was bidden silently to take it to the dustbin. Thus, the haughtiness of the scarlet-jacketed equestrians. All changed when Mandy, my sister competed there, about which much later.

We boys toured all the pavilions and tried to get samples – small boxes of Kellogg's Corn Flakes, tiny bars of Palmolive soap, minute tubes of Pepsodent toothpaste – Pepsodent is also a product Cole Porter lists amongst the items in *You're the Top*. The samples were cherished and swapped. This tour preceded visiting the funfair which only opened at noon. How far would our pocket money take us? Some stalls and rides were compulsory. Fishing paper fish with magnets. A prize guaranteed with each cast of the rod. The prize for the whale was a pump action pellet gun. We all lusted after it. Year after year it stayed there and as we grew older we realised that the stand-holder had no whale amongst the myriad paper fish on the wide plywood trestle table at all. Then we did not fish any more – we had won enough Chappies, trinkets and rubber balls. The shooting range to knock over the tin ducks. Dodgem cars. If there was enough pocket money left, the centrifuge. Bodies stuck against the fast- rotating wall. The wall of death: motorbikes careening round a tubular wall. Mom accompanied us until we were big enough to ride our bikes from Oaklands to Parktown for the Show in the morning when we did not have to queue.

I have kept all my enamel badges. Wearing the tasteful enamel badge in your lapel gave you a distinct feeling of superiority even though few other attendees knew its treasured significance.

Next on the calendar was Guy Fawkes. We started building a bonfire a week before 5 November. We begged and stole fabric and burlap and sisal bags to make a guy to burn on it. Its eyes were Roman Candles, its nose, sparklers, its hands Chinese crackers. Neighbourhood boys, the Martin twins, Caroline Serrurier, the Stewarts joined us. We gathered as far away as possible from the house on the bottom lawn under the cypress tree where Wayne and I planted a plank for the Roman Candles and the Fire Fountains and the crackers we had bought at Norwood

Hardware. All were pooled. Each of us had a turn to light one. "Light blue fuse and stand well back". Strike the match firmly and don't let it fall into the box of crackers. The excitement and anticipation built up over the days before. I carefully counted and calculated the spread of my pocket money. Each cracker had an explosive and a display value, the highest being the rockets. I could never afford more than two 6d. rockets which just fizzed and went up a hundred feet. The Ronden bangers were sold in packets of ten at 1/6d. I ended up with two rockets, a Roman Candle, ten bangers, a ground spinner and a packet of sparklers. I never bought Chinese crackers: they were expensive and burn out their little bangs in seconds. The Babbs' display blended in with other families shooting their rockets into the sky nearby as soon as the sun went down. "There goes a half- crown rocket. And look, a five-bob one!" Giving the monetary value was the only way to express my awe and admiration. Dad did not approve. "You shouldn't say how much they cost," he said sternly. How else was I able to show wonderment? *We* never had a five-bob rocket.

The artisanal nature of our guy which we burnt near the compost pit meant it was never a success. The wood did not burn well, the stuffing would not catch fire and the crackers we had wasted on the effigy did not go off. The whole Guy Fawkes performance was all over in half an hour. The adults repaired to the sitting room (not the lounge, which was non-U) for a whisky as reward for their indulgence. We ran about all the roads in the suburb looking for rocket sticks to collect and treasure.

Guy Fawkes is not long before Christmas. Mom got Johannes Ramagalies to cut two low branches off a deodar and bound them together with wire to make a six-foot tree. The Christmas decorations stayed in a special box in the hall cupboard. Mom fussed over them like a mother hen. The *summum nec plus ultra* was the American tree: big metallic tinsel balls hung on the low branches growing smaller till the silver star on the top. No vulgar plastic baubles, no angels but the odd glass cherry and striped walking stick. Then, the electric lights were wound round the tree and plugged in. Would they work? One blown bulb meant they all stopped as the electricity circuit passed in series.

Rush on your bike to Norwood Hardware to buy a replacement. Did they have coloured bulbs? Over it all Mom hung strings of tinsel.

Until we were teenagers and had long stopped believing in Father Christmas, we had a long, woollen stocking attached to the end of our beds. Puzzles, locks, birds that dipped their heads in a glass and came erect again, packs of cards, comic books and Smarties filled the stockings. The toe always contained an orange. All the best presents under the tree were wrapped in brown paper – bicycles, pellet guns, torches, tents. Emily and Philemon Nyati and Caroline Legae came for their presents: clothes, hats, money, skin-lightening cream.

For a couple of years, when he was chairman of Parkview Golf Club, after opening the presents, Dad took us boys to the golf club where a bucketful of half-crowns was thrown as Christmas presents to the massed caddies causing brawls and unseemly fights and tears from the smaller ones. My father stopped this Christmas tradition which had run for as long as anyone could remember. The coins the next year were handed to each of the caddies, big and small, who lived in the caddies' dormitories on the course. At Lincoln College, Oxford, as penitence for killing a choirboy, the boys of St Michael's parish gather on Ascension Day to scrabble for pennies thrown from the balcony "in perpetuity". The Senior Common Room, early on, began to heat the pennies almost red-hot to burn the boys' fingers. They became wise to this when I went up to Lincoln and arrived with oven gloves, asbestos gloves and scoops to put the hot pennies into canvas bags.

Mom played the conductor's Christmas role in the kitchen as chef with two sous-chefs: ham cooked in beer ("rather undercooked than dry, ten minutes per pound in all" her typed recipe card instructs the cook); turkey with sage, bacon, onion and giblet stuffing, coleslaw, Brussel sprouts, gravy with sherry, roast potatoes. The final *pièce de resistance* rounding the lunch off was the Christmas pudding, brought flaming with brandy into the dining room, tickeys and tanners and, one year, gold charms secreted in its plush innards and served with brandy butter, on which Judd's little frame feasted. Having eaten more brandy butter than pudding, he became distinctively unsteady on his feet after which he went and slept in the Christmas present tent we had erected on the top lawn.

Some friends ate Christmas feasts with us, like Roger Gee, Wayne's best friend, the Windsors whose son Robert was my age, but a pair who were a permanent feature was Greta and Norman Wedgewood. This was a friendless couple. He was taken in by Dad at the golf course and he and his wife were always invited to any dinner, cocktail, buffet or braaivleis the old folks arranged. Shame: we should have felt sorry for Greta. She was a war bride. Saved from penury, misery and destitution by Norman who was part of the British army invading Czechoslovakia at the end of the Second World War. Even after ten years in South Africa she spoke halting English with a heavy accent and Mom was her only friend. We were used to handing the receiver to Mom saying, "It's Greta" and Mom's eyes rose to the heavens. Mom always took the call, and we knew she would be on the line for at least an hour. Greta was childless and the Wedgewoods lived in a charmless flat in Berea. They brought a bottle of champagne to the feast and Greta cut up a peach and stirred it into her champagne glass, ridding it of bubbles. The glasses were round champagne glasses not the flutes universally used now. The flat glasses had been formed to imitate the perfect shape of Marie Antoinette's breasts. We waited in anticipation after the cork had popped and stared fascinated at this annual ritual while we drank our glasses of water. Waifs and strays were Mom's speciality, both animal and human. Though from Greta's mouth I never heard anything interesting – I should have asked her about escaping the Nazis and Czechoslovakia: too late now.

The diminishing asset of HE Babb & Son after Grandpop extracted his very last penny from it and retired to St Michael's on Sea with Peggy, put further strain on my father's finances. What to do? Not a dynamic man, he did not overexert himself for his principals – that was how Judd turned the business around and he also got new principals like Lee Jeans to keep up with the   times. The City Council of Johannesburg had begun permitting "densification" of living spaces and sub-division of erven. Everywhere in the late 50s plots which were topographically amenable to it were being divided up into what the Joburgers called "panhandles" to describe the shape of divided property. Our two acres with a house far from the street lent itself to making a panhandle. The old man applied for planning permission from the municipality to sub-divide and the lower plot sold quickly because of the allure of the Northern suburbs. Along came the land-surveyors with their theodolites and long measuring tapes and hammered in the boundary pegs which cut off the bottom lawn and the *Cedri deodarae* for ever. For ever. No more fêtes, sports days, birthday parties, zinc-tub races on its sloping grass. The pegs also marked a line through mom's favourite garden bed where she had planted agapanthus, daffodils, hollyhocks, leucanthemums, asters, phlox (what a lovely- looking word) and other perennials. This would not do. She resented losing the other half of the garden but her favourite bed? Never. She and Wayne carefully moved the pegs two yards towards the bottom lawn and the drive. They made sure the pegs were aligned and at right angles to the further border. She knew that moving boundary pegs illegally was an offence in terms of the Land Survey Act of 1927, but, no matter. She was prepared to go to jail to keep the garden bed she had tended with her own (and Johannes') hands for a quarter of a century. Standing in her twin-set jerseys, she anxiously watched the fencing company erecting the diamond mesh wire along the new boundary line and worried lest the two extra yards of fencing would alert them to the misdeed. The workers merely cut off the excess and left, and Mom went inside and poured herself a whisky and soda.

The new neighbours were the Tepersons, a young Jewish family manufacturing haberdashery and clothing accessories. Zips, fastening hooks, press-studs, hooks and eyes, buttons and buckles. In similar business to my father. But such was the resentment that someone else was living on our land, that no-one in the family warmed to them or invited them round. The house the Tepersons built was a nondescript ranch-style abode with a raised bedroom. Picture windows were the feature of this style, so we teenagers could observe Mrs Teperson dressing and undressing in her bedroom just beyond the fence to our workshop. Then she had a baby and the nappies waved on the clothesline.

The subdivision of 17 Park St came just before the boys began to shake out their feathers to leave the nest. Flying kites stopped because the Tepersons owned the bottom lawn. The mud hut we had built lay in the way of our new driveway. Wayne had taken it over to breed rabbits to sell to Wits University's zoology and medical faculties and now it lay razed to the ground. Gone were the *Cedri deodarae* which we prayed the Tepersons would not cut down. The bantams still roosted in the mulberry trees and crowed to Rosemary Serrurier's impotent fury. We still had the braaivleis lawn and the swimming pool. But the boys were getting itchy feet.

Wayne started it. Hardly had he got his driving licence when he bought a scrap Austin 10. Outside the workshop there was enough space between us and the Tepersons to park the spoke-wheeled and raise it on brick. He graduated from Dad's scanty toolbox into having the box and flat spanners, the vices, the clamps, the callipers, the gorilla pliers and the screwdrivers neatly on the workbench. The two younger brothers watched with open mouths how oil was drained from the sump, the pistons taken out of the block and the big end bearings replaced on the crankshaft. He painted it a daffodil yellow and he did get it to run, but without a roadworthy licence it could only go on the road surreptitiously and illegally. To see him and the red-headed Roger Gee push-starting it down our new driveway filled Judd and me with envy. Wayne had a mechanical bent and he was at Wits University studying engineering.

He had been the last to fruitfully use the bottom lawn before the subdivision when he invited the engineering faculty to build their float for the Rag on the lawn. Scores of students clambered over the flat-bed truck driven on to the lawn. For testosterone-filled teenagers what an awesome sight to see girls in scanty clothes holding hands with the male students, mounting the float and smoking and drinking wine. The student team worked through the night and painted the float they had built with plywood and canvas. Then the rain came down. All the paint ran. I cannot remember the theme of the float but at nine o'clock bleary-eyed students drove the sodden mass down the lawn and into Park St, with its crew now in their costumes, and headed for the centre of town for the Rag.

Now we were behind the Teperson's wall and the space next to the workshop was where the elder two boys spent time with vehicle parts, generators, starter motors, spark plugs and piston rods, only leaving the workshop for supper. Turpentine to wash off the grease and oil. When Grannie Nina died, the converted garage became Wayne's lair.

As the older boys matured, you could feel an air of restlessness. Wayne was ready for flight. He had moved into the grannie flat in the converted garage and now bought a roadworthy car to replace the daffodil-yellow Austin 10. He bought a black and white Hillman with a sun-roof which gave him autonomy and freedom.

One Saturday morning, he and Roger Gee drove Mom and Mandy to "the Village" – Norwood – to go to the shops. The streets, all named after the offspring of the original owner in Norwood, had no stop street intersections then. At the corner of Algernon and Fanny Roads a woman drove into the side of the Hillman and turned it over, trapping and crushing Mom's body at chest level between the sunroof and the tar. The crash projected Mandy through the sunroof into a barbed wire fence across the sidewalk knocking her out and cutting a long gash across her cheek and down her neck. The two strong youths clambered out of the car and were able to lift the car off Mom and extract her from the wreck. She was badly hurt and broke eleven ribs, a collarbone and shoulder. Dad rushed her to the Norman clinic in Doornfontein where she stayed two weeks recovering. A friend of the family, Mrs Tunbridge, took the badly bleeding Mandy, who was sitting dazedly on the houseowner's stoep, off to the same clinic. Here the medic, as he stitched her up, told her the cut had missed her jugular vein by millimetres and the wound could have killed her.

This took a lot of the oomph out of Mom. She was much subdued after this accident and even her enthusiasm for the Rosebank Booking Service suffered a decline. Fewer dinner parties, fewer cocktail parties, fewer bridge evenings. The parties arranged at home were now teenage parties with bopping till midnight, non-alcoholic punch 33 1/3 records of Chubby Checker, Bobby Darren, Li'l Richard and Elvis Presley. Gilbert Burbach told me how he had pissed into some punch his mother had prepared.

Fortunately, for Mom, there was Mandy. Her care and attention to Mandy kept her spirits up as she slowly got back to her old cheerful and untrammelled psyche. The broken bones were surely a forerunner to the stroke she later had in 1969. But she was now more of a bystander to the development of her sons. Wayne matriculated first class and went daily off to Wits University to study engineering. He began to sow his wild oats and the social life gave him a wholly new experiences. I was in full puberty and in awe of my elder brother's athletics performance which I could never match, exert myself and train as I might. Judd was the happiest in his own skin. The world in which he lived was one of carefree liberty in which he, the Martin twins, David Potter, Mike Matthews and John Piguet, chaffed the birds, sneaked a smoke and avoided any scholastic humdrummery.

In 1960, Mom was able, after all these decades, to visit the Europe she had lived in shortly in her own teens. For an obscure reason, she teamed up with a woman as a companion whom no-one in the family knew and who turned out to be fully anally retentive and the subject of Judd's justified and scornful ribaldry. With this female, Judd and Mandy flew to London, Paris, Rome, Florence and Lake Como. This gave the family a new expression: often using tourist coaches to get around, Judd and Mandy put on the multilingual earphones to hear the running commentary on the sights. In his impish way, Judd changed Mandy's language channel to which Mandy cried: "Don't press my French!" Any annoying action by a child from then on, was met with: "Don't press my French!"

The boys began to leave the nest. Wayne was employed by Everite and then sent to Port Elizabeth by the Exide Battery company. The converted garage was rented out to an odd assortment of tenants, one of whom was busted for stealing appurtenances from the mansions being razed on Parktown ridge to make way for the new Johannesburg General Hospital designed by Hannes Meiring, which he admitted as being "a youthful mistake" because it resembled a Boer War blockhouse.

After a year in Sixth Form at St John's, I set off for Stellenbosch University accompanied by Mom and my devoted fox terrier, Drummer, in the wheezing and unreliable Austin A40 I had bought, breaking down at both Bultfontein and Beaufort West on the 1,800km trip. So, for Wayne and me, 17 Park Street became less a home and more a reliable base to stay in, to use for its swimming bath and to be sure of a meal. Judd had entered HE Babb & Son and was also seeking his independence. He had long ago learned to drive and he, David Potter and Mike Matthews nightly quietly took the blue Chev (a Fleetliner) down the drive to go on evening jaunts. This included driving as fast as possible down African Street to get the exhilarating high (or low) of the dip at the bottom of the hill. Dad expressed horror that the bonnet of the car had been prised open at the hinges. "Somebody tried to break into the car," he exclaimed, and we all came to look, Judd looking as though butter would not melt in his mouth, knowing that the bonnet's catch had sprung open at the infamous dip and that the bonnet had bent back against the windscreen. The chums had silently restored the car to the driveway and tiptoed away to their homes.

In the three and a half decades the family stayed in Park Street, only one criminal act affected us. The boundary to the road was a double strand of wire between steel posts. The front door was seldom locked, there were only a few windows covered by burglar bars. One night, Dad woke up to see his trousers, cleverly plucked from his closed trouser press, disappearing on a long bamboo rod out of the bedroom window. He shouted but knew not to clutch the long pole because the burglars stuck razorblades into the bamboo. He ran to the front door, but the agile thief had disappeared down the drive, trousers and rod in both hands.

Mandy continued to lie under the standard lamp in the sitting room (not the lounge, which was non-U) immersed in one book after the other, the direct light helping her eyes to read. The Scott bird lithograph, the convex mirror, Faed's homely scene and the young woman continued working on her tapestry and the winklepicker still had his back to us. Dad moved to Texan cigarettes without filters and constantly spat out the bits of loose tobacco or delicately picked them off his tongue. Mom now smoked double-filter Peter Stuyvesants. The *le petit train-train* of life followed its comfortable trajectory. The dogs changed and now the semicircle around the hearth included a Dalmatian, a borzoi, a bastard poodle called Passepartout and a fox terrier. The inner semicircle had a tabby, a black cat and a Siamese called Renoy because that is how Emily Nyati rendered the onomatopoeia of her strangled meow. The cats still reliably followed Mom's tinkling gold bracelet to the pantry, rubbing against her legs, meowing and looking appealingly up at her when she prepared their evening supper and distributed the sugar and tea for the servants. The virile rambunctiousness of male teenagers steadily reduced and at the dining table the numbers dropped to four and then three.

Once I had left for Stellenbosch, 17 Park Street hosted me only at holidays. Judd, after his marriage to Judy, lived in the converted garage for a short while till he hired a house in Norwood and Wayne was far away. When I was at Oxford, after I went down, and on home leave I stayed with my in-laws at Douglasdale, the site of Douglasdale Dairies, now sub-divided into large plots. My last photograph of the house shows the three boys, Mandy, Judd and Judy, a little St John and Bridie in a cot on the bank behind the pool. It was almost a doomed pool, because during that visit, I noticed the absence of St John and immediately ran to the swimming pool and there he was, his hair spread out like a waterlily pad in the water. I dived in and held him up and what sounded like a laugh came from his little mouth. It was a gasp, a medic told me. We almost did not have a doctor of Celtic languages in the family. That was my last stay at 17 Park Street. The communal platform which had launched us faded like a distant earth seen from an Apollo rocket.

After the boys had left and I had begun my first diplomatic posting in Paris, the old folk sold 17 Park Street and moved to "the Village" – well, hardly: Mom would not have downsized to the *hokkies* in the Village near Grant Avenue. They chose a house at 62 Osborne Road, Norwood. Osborne was the owner of the whole of Norwood who named the streets after his children. The house they chose lay opposite Houghton Golf course on a triangular corner plot with Cecile Street running right next to the house, unusual for Joburg which demanded a set back from the road. That the crime here was different was soon apparent. Umbrellas left by guests at a dinner party at the front door all disappeared during the supper. Mandy refused to live in the room which gave direct access to the sidewalk from which pedestrians had a good view into the room. The house was big enough to have servants' quarters and Emily and Philemon moved there, too.

The old folk lived in a caravan on the property while builders knocked down walls and altered it more to Dad's liking than to Mom's. It was at 62 Osborne Road that Mom was diagnosed with breast cancer and had her right breast removed. She submitted herself to the devastating, dreadful and useless chemotherapy during which she continued to write to me and Ann in Paris. She wrote in her firm, even, round and neat unchanging handwriting in Royal Blue Parker ink with which she filled her medium nib fountain pen, on Basildon Bond airmail paper and sent in a Basildon Bond airmail envelope. Unfailingly she used the self-deprecatory "*j* " rather than capital "I." Nothing daunted, in her last letters she gave news of her generation of friends I knew. After congratulating me on my promotion to Second Secretary, she says:

> "We as a family are not very good at expressing our deeper emotions but here I must tell you how very proud I am of you ...

> "Mandy tells me that Chris Everett got married a week ago to Iona Ramsay. I don't know if I told you I saw them at the Volck

wedding? It sounds unkind, but I have to say he looked rather like an armpit! Pale, pasty skin & straggly hair all over his face & neck. Not the nice-looking lad I remember at school. Iona was taken away from Kingsmead as she was psychologically unfitted there & was unhappy. Good match!! ... "Saturday we had dinner with the Hancox. The McClurgs were the other guests. 9.30 came & Peter stood up saying: 'Well, you can all go now. I'm tired and I'm going to bed' He fades quite quickly."

Her next letter in February 1972 is the second last I received. After saying she "developed a small colony of micro-dot lumps on the chest and the arm swelled up again ... was given a cocktail of injections plus another lot of pills. I am to go in 3 wks time again" she speaks of her excitement of coming to see us in Paris. She says: "I won't be a nuisance to you I hope as I can do an awful lot I couldn't do even a few months ago. Can't do up my bra or wash under my right arm! Can walk to the "to-to" and look after myself etc. so no more intimate worries any more."

This is when Mom had a stroke. She fell out of bed. Dad said he would take her to the hospital in the morning. At that stage, the medical world had not woken up to the urgency of treating a stroke as soon as possible to remove the constriction in veins. Medical help came too late and she was paralysed down her right side. No rehabilitation was going to help her get movement on that side again.

From Paris, where I was serving as Third Secretary in the South African Embassy, I came on home leave to find my mother a ghost of her old self. She never stopped trying. Above all she "didn't want to be a nuisance". I have the last letter she wrote with her paralysed hand, held by the other, in which the words slope and wiggle but her courage is still matchless. It is written, as usual, with the fountain pen on Basildon Bond in Royal Blue ink and she had even written out the address on the airmail envelope. Her concerns are with Mandy and the doomed visit to Paris. She even walked a little holding on to me in Rosebank where she saw a Delft plate in a shop window. She gazed at it a moment, but the shop was shut. The next day I went to buy it. It was plastic, but

I got it anyway. The faithful Anton drove her around everywhere. She would not stay at home. She was restless and furious at the trick fate had played on her. She was trapped in this mutilated frame. She could not admit her frailty and incapacity. To her huge embarrassment and shame, she defecated on the physiotherapist's shoes .

St Martin's-in-the-Veld filled up to the rafters with Joburgers she had known and with flowers in every nook and cranny for her funeral. As she had said to me when her mother died, "would you not cry?" I did throughout the service and was consoled by Caroline Legae and Emily Nyati outside the stone church – they had known her almost as long as I. Dad said, before we took our places in the front pew: "Strange combination" – I was wearing my brown pin-striped double-breasted Yves St Laurent suit with dark blue shirt – "must have got them in Paris." I had arrived on UTA that very morning. The other brothers had lived close to the decline in her mien and the weakening of the body and spirit and had been mourning for much longer. They were more composed and calmer, but Mandy was profoundly pole-axed by Mom's death. Even her newfound church friends could not raise her devastated spirits.

That afternoon, all the siblings foregathered at 62 Osborne Road in Norwood and started going through Mom's things. She had twenty-three twinsets which we took out of her cupboard to give to Caroline Legae and Emily Nyati. "And what about me?" Mandy lamented sadly. Oops! We redivided them and described to Mandy the colours and shades so she could select some for herself. She was identical in height and size as Mom. Judd took the pastel drawing of white roses on the green background that she had drawn during rehabilitation classes. It is stunning. She could have been a great artist, a great creator: instead, she was an administrator, an organiser also of her children.

I stayed with Judd and Judy and left in a huge void. The emptiness was broad and deep. As she had said, we, as a family, had difficulty in expressing our deeper emotions. I do not think any of us said to another "I love you" or held hands or put arms around another. We stood up when adults entered the room. We waited till the grown-ups were served before eating. I never heard Mom complaining when Dad came back late from golf. The only spanking I remember was for opening the medicine chest. The medicine chest only contained Anadin, aspirin, Philips Milk of Magnesia, mercurochrome, iodine, Syrup of Figs, castor oil, Elastoplast and, Dad's standby, Carter's Little Liver Pills (tiny white balls) so no-one was going to do themselves much harm consuming that pharmacopeia. Not even ENO's got to our medicine cabinet:

"E _ N _O, ENO,
When you're feeling low:
ENO.
It's kind and gentle
And good, good tasting
E_N_O"

The motto was "get on with it", "keep buggering on" and "pull yourself together". No one else was going to do it for you. And that is what all the children did in reverence to their mother. Her legacy to us.

The old man and Mandy stayed on at 62 Osborne Road and Dad was now a fifty-nine-year- old widower. Mandy tells me that he was now prey for the widows and divorcees of their set. The phone rang constantly of an evening and Mandy was taking messages from Beryl, from Pat, from Olivia but especially from Ruth.

Ruth Foley, widow of Arthur Foley, an insurance broker had lived in Melrose and then moved to The Valley Road in Westcliff, the *nec plus ultra* of upper class Joburg. She was a Glenton. Fred Glenton together with a young Mitchell whom his bride had met on the voyage over from England, started Glenton & Mitchell's, a coffee and tea distribution business that was flourishing and almost monopolistic. It packed FG Coffee (named after Fred Glenton) and PG Tips Tea (named after Peter Glenton) but had made its name with Joko Tea, publicised by a tea wagon in the livery of a Joko tea packet pulled by two ponies, Jo and Ko, leaving fans of Joko all over South Africa. Fred Glenton had learnt about tea while laying linoleum in a grocery store in England and, thinking Mitchell was rich, while in fact his only capital was a loan of £1000 from an uncle in Ireland, had asked him to partner him a venture of importing quality Ceylon tea and selling it on after packaging to schools, hospitals and mines. The firm started in Jeppestown in Joburg and moved to Craighall Park near to the Rand Show in 1972. It now belongs to Lipton's.

Our families mixed often when Ruth and Arthur lived in Melrose. They had three children, the eldest, a girl, Trish; Fred, named after his grandfather, a year older than Wayne and Tim, my age. Kids of our ilk went to Limberlost, a nursey school, which we called "Mrs Ward's" because Mrs Ward owned and ran it. It was not far from the Foley home. After school I was often with Tim, but he had the habit of dressing up in his sister's dresses and trailing me behind him as "the prince" which made me unwilling to walk there after school. Mom played tennis there and, watching the white-skirted ladies swatting the tennis ball, I concluded that the aim of the sport was to see how high you could hit the tennis court fence. The Foleys' daughter became a truck driver in Rhodesia. Fred was an uncontrollable, rambunctious, large and violent boy who went first to Parktown Prep School and on reaching puberty, as a boarder, to Michaelhouse, the school to which all parents aspired to send their sons. His noisy and aggressive behaviour came from the Irish genes. He certainly scared us with his physical strength and loud voice.

But here's the thing: Ruth presided over a dysfunctional brood but it did not help that she was a martinet while Arthur faded unnoticed into the background. She did the most appalling thing. To overcome Fred's undisciplined character, Ruth decided to have him lobotomised at the age of seventeen. It was the "cure" for Hollywood's Lana Turner, so why not for Fred? Fred was calm thereafter to the point of vegetativeness and the only job he could procure was sanitising public telephone booths. And this was the woman who was to marry my father. It sends shivers up my spine. Lobotomy, cutting the brain off from all sentiments and feelings. She did it to her own child.

Tim went to the States and became a butler to leading families. On his return he lived in Auckland Park and was murdered in his bed during an armed robbery.

With her fortune and overbearing personality, it did not take long for her to hook the old man. She came to live at 62 Osborne Road and Mandy moved out after Ruth had shouted at her: "If you can't come for dinner on time you won't get dinner!' at which Mandy picked up her plate and went to her room never to dine with Ruth again. She hired her own flat and with her guide dog went to live in Yeoville, quite prepared and brave enough to face the world alone. Perhaps that was one favour that Ruth did her. When Mandy was told Ruth had died, her response was: "Good!"

Ruth soon found superior accommodation in Melrose and bought an Edwardian house in Reform Road. She took Dad on a world cruise, but it was soon clear to her that the old man was not the cavalier, swashbuckling swain of his youth. Her controlling and haughty manner by comparison with Dad's laid-back fecklessness could only end unhappily. We saw this when they stopped over in Paris where I was serving, had them for dinner and took them to characteristic Paris bistros.

> A word on bistros: the word is Russian. After the Germans and Russians besieged Paris in 1871, the Russians occupied all the cafés where they shouted to the inn-keeper "Bistro! Bistro!" Quick, quick! This became the generic term for light meal establishments. It has continued into the American invasion in 1945; scattered all over Paris are "Quicks" a shortening of the American "quick service".

Ruth broke her hip on steps in Paris and spent two weeks in Salpétrière Hospital at France's expense. She shared a two-bed ward with a long-suffering Frenchwoman and soon began smoking twenty cigs a day much to the distress of the fellow patient and driving the nurses to distraction. Rules did not apply to Ruth. Shortly after the cruise, the marriage dissolved and Dad went to live at the Old Johannian Club in Linksfield of which he had been chairman. There was a cottage on the grounds and, there, Dad spent the last healthy days of his life, playing bowls on the impeccably mowed greens of the Club.

Each evening he repaired to the Club bar and ordered his whisky and soda. The Club Secretary, Bill Dalton, was friendly and indulgent to dad until he, too, had a debilitating stroke. Bill Dalton had a brass plaque screwed onto the bar where Dad sat: "Babb's Bend."

When cancer debilitated him, he took no medical advice and saw no medic. One day, when his weakness had become intolerable, he drove, somehow, his battered BMW to Walkerville where Wayne was living and pitched up without warning. It was there that I saw him for the last time. Warned by Wayne that our 72-year-old father was close to popping his clogs, I flew from Ottawa where I was serving and spent a couple of days watching an unseeing, half-conscious father being fed and helped to the loo by Dimph, Wayne's intensive care nurse- wife. He repeatedly said: "It'll all come right." He spent his last days in a hospice living under sedation in the spirit of "keep buggering on"' until he could not any more. He could not keep buggering on.

Three Boys

Three boys in khaki

Three boys were born to the marriage. Then came Mandy and she deserves a chapter all on her own. Mom had so badly wanted a girl that we were all called "Amanda" before we came mewling and puking into the world. Because I am writing this, of course the story of our upbringing and growing up comes to life through my eyes. It could not be otherwise. I do not apologise. I shall paint it warts and all and only as I saw it.

I was the second boy. The middelmannetjie. This middle position in the family is on its way to extinction as fertility declines and families of three or more become a rarity in the West. Since the time of the psychologist, the acolyte of Sigmund Freud, Arthur Adler, the studies of the middle child have proliferated. He believed that the order of your birth affected your character and your psychology. The stereotype of the middle child depicts the child as neglected by his parents as their attention veers to the first-born who formerly had the monopoly of care and they indulge the youngest. So, the middle child seeks attention, feels neglected and becomes embittered. Apart from the last-mentioned characteristic, Katrin Schumann and Catherine Schmidt found that the stereotype was remarkably accurate, but their study and others thereafter conclude that the characteristics have a positive outcome. Their book is optimistically titled: *The Secret Power of Middle Children* and this gives a cheerful result to the middle order in the family. As to characteristics, the studies show that the middle infant has to become self-sufficient, even non-conformist, and organised in self-defence against the natural dynamics of the family. It also means such child is resilient but also a born negotiator: he is the one who resolves disputes as the one in the middle of everything, smooths over disagreements and is a natural negotiator – a diplomat. The authors mourn the fact that this type of person is disappearing to the detriment of innovation and non-conformity.

It was uncomfortable being in the middle and I never got over the impression that Wayne was Dad's and Judson Mom's favourite, so I had to try harder. Wayne was born on 12 July 1939, Glenn on 4 June 1943 and Judson on 15 October 1945. Amanda came when I was eight and Judd six, on 11 September 1951. We all got at least two Christian names: Anthony Wayne – I never asked where the Anthony came from, but Mom said they tried Wayne Anthony and the rhythm and the initials seemed wrong, so, Anthony Wayne it was. I got Glenn Robin Ware, Glenn the Americanism, Robin was one of Mom's swains, Robin Summers, a photographer whose son, Sean, became CEO of Pick n Pay – "Piss and Poo", as Mandy called it – and Ware, the maiden name of Horace's first wife and Dad's mother; Judson Hugh the Americanism plus his uncle's name; and then Amanda (at last!) plus Nina, Mom's mother, plus Maude, Dad's mother.

Glenn was not a common name and, as a boy, I mockingly was called Glynis or Glenise. It came as a bit of a relief when my family nickname became "Gum" because Mandy's infant tongue could not manage Glenn; Wayne, for the same reason, became "Um", and Juddy, "Dutchie". No-one at school shared our forenames. Today, the Cape Flats is filled with Glenns and Waynes; no Judsons, though.

Wayne had had the full attention of his parents for almost four years. It can only have been a nuisance to have this newcomer spoil the fun.

The four-year distance made an alliance of boyhood unlikely and so it was. But my earliest memory was of Judd. Such early memories at two-year's old are said to be *ex post facto* suggestions adopted as memories. No-one could have suggested my being picked up by Mom to look through the glass in the Florence Nightingale nursery at a bundled-up baby held by a nurse. Even the light cast from the window at the end of the passage is vivid. Just a flash in time and captured on the retina of my brain.

From Judd's birth, all the boys were interlinked, but rivals. Rivals. The psychologists are right – the middle ones have to share. They don't get the separate bedroom. I told the story of the Leng Dixon paintings on our bedheads. Why do you always feel you're pulling the short straw? Not true, but that's how it seems. Wayne, the elder, the big boy, was neat, organised. His toys were put away neatly. He put his Lionel train set away in its box neatly. He stored his toys on the cupboard shelf neatly. He neatly took photographs of his toys arranged on the top lawn, all in neat condition. Don't sneak in and borrow one: he'll know and find you pushing his Dinky cars over the carpet and snatch them from you. Judd was always happy in his own skin. Little perturbed him. He had an ease of behaviour that didn't brook interference. His toys were shared with me in higgledy-piggledy trunks.

We grew up rivals. Mom did not oppose it. She naturally did not encourage it but often had to separate us and end arguments. But it still puzzles me that she never, never encouraged us to watch one another's back. So, what happened at home, continued at school. Never did the old folks say: "You must stand up for each other. You must help each other." The rivalry was expected, and the rambunctiousness and fractiousness permeated through our youth. An alliance between the eldest and the youngest was a natural result and you know the old saying: "the only thing that gets sharper with use is the tongue," that is what happened with me and frustratingly and unpleasantly I used crass, jejune words to cut away at the others: *ad hominem* remarks, especially as a teen. Insults about ears, teeth, skin. Juvenile and petty.

Mom certainly saw me as a bright child, and I went to kindergarten from three years old. There was a monster that lived with me. A monster that never got off my shoulder until I was almost thirty: migraine. I inherited it from Mom. Almost every ten days of my life the monster appeared. It started small. First tiny blind spot appeared in my vision. That was when I almost went limp from fear and loathing. The spot grows, blinds more and works its way to the edge of your eyesight, little crosses shimmering and dancing teasingly across your line of sight. It grows and unsights you until it mockingly fades behind your eyelids leaving behind a throbbing, unfocusing veil. That is just the warning. You anticipate the next phase. You retch. There is bit of relief. The you retch again until you think your stomach must be empty. Then you retch up green bile. It burns your throat. Surely this is the end? No, there is more green bile with the next retch. When the yellow bile sears and rasps your throat and mouth, you know you are near the end of the vomiting. Maybe one more stinging yellow spit. The pain in your forehead begins. It lies against your skull. It presses. It cruelly sears into all your consciousness. Your head is now splitting. No, not splitting. An iron band pushes your skull outwards. There is no relief. It is unending. Then you are so exhausted that you fall into a troubled sleep. When you wake, you are fuzzy. Your fingertips are numb. Your tongue is fat and unmoving. You slur your words. This is the loneliest affliction. You are on your own and there is no comfort in it. No icepack. No water. You feel that if you were to drink or eat anything you would sick it up. Any pill you take is vomited up. Only once, when Bridget McClurg gave me AP Cod (codeine, I suppose) at the first signs, did the retching and the headache not follow. Miracle. It was only when Dr Johan Gerber, Thijs Nel's friend, recommended Neurofen that this torture came to an end. From then, capture the vision deformation in time, and the horrors do not swivel in your head.

The first migraine came at kindergarten at three year' old. Because Mom thought I was clever, she farmed me out to a nursery school in 2nd Avenue, Abbotsford. One day, here I vomited and the carers crossly took me outside and sat me in the gutter outside the gate and went to phone

Mom. I was sick another couple of times when Johannes Ramagalies rides down the road on his bike. Mom did not seem to be at home, so Emily had despatched Johannes to my rescue. He sat me on the crossbar and pedalled back home, but as he turned into Park Street, a foot got caught in the spokes of his wheel. More suffering made worse by an old biddy who shouted over her wall that I should not cry. Up through the deodars to home where Emily put me to bed with a potty to be sick in. My first migraine.

The fecklessness of that kindergarten moved Mom to put me in another more sophisticated kindergarten attached to the Methodist Church in Cradock Avenue in Rosebank. There were three classes, and I was the youngest child at the school. I was often left uncomprehending of how things worked. Incidents of this early socialisation recur and trouble me. Near Christmas, children were asked to bring clothes and toys "for the poor". To entertain us, the teachers let us each take one item to our desks. I took a book and was peering at the pictures when it came time to gather them together for packing up "for the poor". I grasped the edges of the book and fought hard not to release this treasure. With a laugh and with their greater strength, the teachers snatched the book away. Tears and frustrated anger. Another nightmare recurs: as I was the youngest, the teachers thought I should not accompany them to some outing and locked me in the classroom. The crying and the tears after their departure was to no avail. I could see some adults playing tennis at the next house. They could rescue me. I appealed, I shouted, I cried. Adults leaving me to such a fate? The door of the classroom at last opened when my sobs had already turned to hiccups and the cold-hearted Hanna let me pick up my satchel and wait with the others for our lifts. Mom was often late. The waiting infants clambered over a pile of branches and twigs and played, careless of injury. Then they were all gone. I was on my own. Frantic – must I run down the road? I could not find my satchel. Stolen by some passer-by. The blue Chev arrived after the tears had welled again over my bottom lids.

By four I was beginning to read with unending curiosity. On the way back from Daggie and Ernest's farm, I asked: "What is 'PTY LTD'?" "It means a company?" That did not explain. "And 'S&L' on the windmill?" "Stewarts and Lloyds, a company". Still puzzling. "And VW?" "Volkswil – the voters." I mulled over this. Rather know the nursery rhymes. And I knew them all read to me by Mom from a Pre-Raphaelite Arthur Rackman compendium. How did he make the fish look as though they were really in the water and blowing bubbles?

Rather know the nursery rhymes. Mom read to me and Judd before supper on the two-seater couch out of an Arthur Rackman compendium with Pre-Raphaelite illustrations: a mouse running down a grandfather clock with an irritated face, Wee Willie Winkie skipping through town in medieval stockinged feet, a market stall with a fat pig staring out of its pen. I knew them all by heart. Less likeable were the sado-masochism stories of the Grimm brothers with creepy stepmothers, cannibalistic witches living in gingerbread cottages. Most awful of all was *Struwwelpieter* who tears wings off flies, lets his hair grow in blond, erect and spiky dreadlocks. This German book contains moral tales of maids lighting matches and burning to ash and inky boys plunged into ink for mocking a black man and a boy fading away to bony skeletal sticks till a soup tureen is placed on his grave: "Take the nasty soup away!" is his refrain.

Fortunately, Mom's sunny Americanism interposed itself. The bookshelf displayed Little Golden Books, half-folio books with a gold-decorated spine. My first dog, Pokey, was named after *The Poky Little Puppy* that went roly-poly down the hill. The morality taught in these tales was upbeat, not Teutonically punitive. *The Little Red Hen:* "Who will help me plant the grain?" "Not I," said the pig. "Not I," said the horse. "Not I," said the cow, "Then I will", said the Little Red Hen. "Who will eat the bread?" "I will!" said the pig. "I will!" said the horse. "I will!" said the cow. "No, I'll do it myself!" said the Little Red Hen. Try and try again, was the motto: *The Little Engine Who Could* and *The Brave Little Steam Shovel*. Simple lessons learnt from *The Colour Kittens*.

The books I liked most, and which had the wryest illustrations were the American *Uncle Wiggily Stories*. Uncle Wiggily was an aging long-eared rabbit who walked with the aid of a crutch "painted like a barber's pole". Each story ended with a condition and a promise: "If the squirrel doesn't drop a pinecone on the muskrat's head, I'll next tell you of Uncle Wiggily and the Laughing Gas Balloons." And sure enough, that was the next story. The muskrat was Uncle Wiggily's minder, Jane Fuzzy Wuzzy. All sorts of creatures populated the Uncle Wiggily's stories. The author, Howard Garis, from 1910 wrote an Uncle Wiggily story every day for 51 years for the *Chicago Tribune* (except for Sundays!) and published 79 books.

Smaller still, were the Beatrix Potter books: *Peter Rabbit*, whose father ended up in Mrs McGregor's pie, but the best was the *Tailor of Gloucester* who frees the mice from under the upturned cups the cat has captured them in. They reward the tailor by sewing the weskit the mayor has ordered with tiny stitches when he falls ill. He has to deliver the weskit on Christmas Day in the morning. They leave pinned on it the almost completed weskit a tiny note: "No more twist!" for the tailor to remedy.

When I read to myself, I devoured the Noddy books, smaller still, all thirty-four of them. Piet Lloyd, my Lower I friend had almost all of them. Why did I like these sappy Enid Blyton stories? It was the rhythm of them. Big Ears, the skittles, Mr Plod the policeman and the wicked golliwogs who later had to be depicted as being green to avoid racial profiling. And the little cat-bell on his hat and the open car. Parp! Parp! Now, the psychologists depict the Big Ears – Noddy relationship as homosexual. Enid Blyton had tomboys in both the Famous Five and Secret Seven books. Odd.

This was concomitant with *Rupert the Bear* whose tales were told under flat coloured illustrations also beginning in the press in the *Daily Express* always accompanied by Pong-Ping the Pekinese dog and the wise best friend, Bill the Badger. And the William books that caused me belly laughs, but just puzzled my children when I read the William stories to them. Richmal Crompton, the author never looked down on her readers, wrote. The vocabulary was what she used as a grown-up. That was the hook: no condescension. William was an eleven-year-old and was pursued by his *amanuensis*, the *nouveau riche* Violet-Elizabeth. "I'll thcweam and thcweam until I'm thick", goes Violet Elizabeth's refrain when thwarted. William and the Outlaws were an unruly lot living in a village near London. William had a dog called Jumble and a pretty sister in her late teens. William could never understand why she was pursued by the swains of the village and did not hesitate to interrupt their intimate moments.

Wayne had progressed by this time to *Popular Mechanics* and *Scientific American* and was planning how to turn the mud hut Judd and I had built, into a breeding room for rabbits to sell to the science laboratory for experiments at Witwatersrand University. He built the mud hut up to above head height and covered it with a proper corrugated iron roof.

Dad taught us golf. A canvas bag, holding ancient clubs, stood in the entrance cupboard. How to hold the club? With your forefinger linked over the pinkie of the right hand and the V of your fist towards your chin. The clubs had names like mashie, niblick, cleek, driver and spoon. Some had wooden shafts. Dad gave us his balls with cuts in them and we chipped on the front lawn and drove down to the bottom lawn. Judd as a pre-teenager could already tee off a ball and drive from the top lawn into Park Street. Dad also invested in books on golf which he referred us to. Arnold Palmer was his favourite. I followed Arnold Palmer's lesson on how to get a ball away from behind a tree and must have misunderstood because I broke one of the wooden shafts against the trunk of the cypress tree at the dining room entrance and guiltily put it in the dustbin. No mashie after that.

Dad did not really have the patience to teach us golf. One holiday he hired a beach house in Natal opposite the Southbroom golf course and took me and Judd to play nine holes. This was an adventure. At the first tee, a three par, both Judd and I reached the green with our first drive. Thereafter, things did not go smoothly, and we were taking seven shots to get to the hole. Dad could not wait to leave the course and offered both of us a lesson with the course professional. The pro did not like the idea of teaching an untalented twelve-year-old and a precocious ten-year-old and did a half-hearted job.

Wayne was less interested in the golf than in the golf balls which he cut up to see the rubber bands curl snappily away from the cutting blade and extract the tiny sac like a balloon containing the liquid resin or rubber at its core.

More persistent was Dad's passion for boxing. He boxed as a boy at St John's and showed symptoms of rheumatic fever after a boxing bout which brought school sports to a shuddering halt for him. Grandpop Horace served on the South African Boxing Board of Control and attended the major fights at Wembley Stadium. Dad arranged for a boxing coach to teach us every Saturday morning. Up the drive came a podgy, balding Irishman, Brian Best, carrying a carpet bag filled with small boxing gloves the size of cushions so no-one would get hurt. Dad and Mom arranged for boys from the neighbourhood to come to boxing classes. The Fulton brothers, also Irish, Robert and John, Robert Windsor, son of an employee of Dad's and other neighbours' boys. After exercises, hitting a punch ball on a spring and jabbing at an upheld gloved hand, Brian Best put us through our paces in sparring with boys of our own size. Keep your left shoulder facing your opponent. Keep your guard up. Jab, the one-two, always lead with your left, the uppercut, the duck and dive. Keep your gloves in front of your face. The Babb boys did not have the killer instinct and remained unaggressive.

Brian Best enrolled us in competitions he promoted all over Joburg: at Marist Brothers College, at Fairs and Exhibitions, at Yeoville School. I have six little silver cups for bouts I won mysteriously, given the routine way I

**Judd and Glenn at 17 Park Street.
These photos stood next to Mom's bed until she died**

boxed. But one cup I definitely deserved. Mom dropped me off one evening at Yeoville School where boxing was a necessity in the rough neighbourhood. I always had butterflies in my stomach in going to these matches. When it was my turn to get into the ring, I saw my opponent for the first time. Brian Best had miscalculated or just guessed because he was more than a foot taller than me and big boned. Then the announcer announced over the loudspeaker that I was from St John's which triggered hoots of derision, whistles and calls of "More pressure in the rear, St John's!" from the Yeoville louts. I was not going to win this popularity contest. As soon as the bell rang for the first round, I flew towards this big boy and started pummelling him in the belly. Because he was taller, he could only hit the top of my head which I kept down. He had to push me away to get a chance of punching me which he did often, but I saw my tactic was working. He had difficulty in hitting my face. The audience was beginning to change sides. Now I heard: "Hit him! Hit him!" "Go, St John's" and I heard laughter and encouragement for the boy the audience had, at the beginning of the bout, consigned to the canvas and an overwhelming victory for Yeoville School. I lost, of course, and the bigger guy had his hand raised by the ref. Brian Best felt guilty for this mismatch and appeared the next Saturday with a silver cup for me. It was engraved: "A GAME LOSER". I treasure that cup for its irony and ambiguity. It is one of my prize possessions.

The Babbs were very convenient for Brian Best. He was also a boxing promoter and engaged the Scots, Peter Keenan and John McAteer, to have

**Brian Best and the boxing group with cushion gloves.
Wayne and John Best at the rear**

bouts in South Africa – Keenan to challenge Vickie Toweel for the world bantamweight championship and McAteer for a lightweight bout. The Toweel brothers, Vick and Willie were local heroes. Vic had won a bronze medal at the Olympics. Peter Keenan and McAteer trained on our top lawn where Brian Best had erected a boxing ring, complete with canvas, and hung a punchbag on a low branch of the plane tree. They went the "All-Scottish" route. Peter Keenan and McAteer always wore kilts and were photographed by the press with tartan shorts and tam o' shanters. They were high-spirited and spent every day in our house, laughing and ribbing each other. Peter Keenan borrowed my BB lever-cocking pellet gun and shot John in the buttocks. For us boys, this was sacrilege. Never point a gun at someone! It was thrilling to see someone break all the rules. The shot stung John McAteer but he immediately laughed and the two wrestled over the gun which they then shot at more innocuous targets.

The SABC broadcast both the bouts. When Peter Keenan climbed into the ring, we three boys sat round the radiogram. We did not know who to cheer for. We knew Peter Keenan and he had entertained us with his Scottish brogue and had treated us with relaxed good humour and friendliness. Vic Toweel was, however, South Africa's champion. We listened in fascination at the back and forth of the bout and had to wait for the result: Vickie had won on points. All three of us were ambivalent in our delight and went to bed knowing the boxing ring on the front lawn would soon be gone and the punchbag unslung from the plane tree.

There is a Willie in Jeremy Taylor's *Ag, Pleez, Daddy*:

> "Ag Pleez, Daddy, won't you take us to the wrestling.
> We wanna see a ou called Sky High Lee.
> When he meets Willie Liebenberg
> There's gonna be a murder
> 'Cos Willie's gonna donner
> That blerrie Yankee!"

Dad did take us to Wembley Stadium to see Vic Toweel box. Grandpop Horace, unusually, invited me up to the seats of the Boxing Board of Control. That did not last long. I shouted for Vickie and Grandpop immediately expelled me out of the neutral corner back to bleachers.

Indispensable for us: a pellet gun; a bicycle - so happy to graduate to a 26-inch wheeler with drop handlebars and three gears from the 24-inch wheels and the straight handlebars. The radio: the radiogram in the sitting-room and 78 rpm records. Listen to Eric Egan before going to school from seven to seven thirty and the Corny Crack at seven fifteen – a quip that was once too suggestive for the SABC Board and Eric Egan was suspended. The cover-up was that he had blown a fuse with the studio electric kettle. Before portable transistor radios the boys gathered round the sitting room radiogram to listen to *The Creaking Door, Consider Your Verdict, Lux Radio Theatre,* and *Sixty Thousand to Go*. On Fridays we listened to the *Quiz Kids* because a St John's boy was on the team, William Torbitt. The school did not usually allow boys to "go public." These were all broadcast at eight o'clock and dinner was from seven to eight, so we never got to hear Mark Saxon or Squad Cars. They clashed with supper, though we sometimes heard the end catchphrase of one of those programmes, like Taxi: "If I don't see ya t'rough da week, I'll see ya t'rough da window."

The bikes got us everywhere. To go skating at Wembley Ice Rink at the Southern end of town where you could hire skates that had braces to hold them to your leg, so old and decrepit were they. I rode to Germiston Lake to yacht with André Carr on his sharpie. We rode to flicks. We rode in convoy

Judd with Caesar, Pokey and Piper

Mandy with Daffy and Puddle

to golf at Huddle Park Golf Course. We rode to the Old Johannian Club in Linksfield. I also rode to school, but Judd and Wayne did not like that idea after Philemon no longer took us in the grey Chev. In winter, that meant putting on a balaclava and gloves and sweating up Third Street and catching onto the pole of the Number 6 bus to get up the last hill before Houghton Drive and catch your breath before the South Col of Munro Drive where it was a matter of pride not to dismount and push the bike up the last steep incline. This meant that I once fainted at bugle practice for that extra effort. I persisted with riding to school because I could see Jill Millner at Houghton School who shyly waited for me in her maroon blazer at the corner of First Avenue to wave as I passed.

Animals crawled all over 17 Park Street. We each had a dog which all lived to ripe old ages. Until Piper, the dalmatian, palmed off on us by the Roseveares for having spots too wide apart, all the dogs were mongrels. Mine was Pokey, a black smooth-haired, tough dog, the size of a spaniel. The name presaged a lot in his life. He roamed the suburb and made friends with all the dogs he met in the street. This annoyed Dr Wolfe's houseman so much that he hurled a poker at it. It entered Pokey's back and protruded six inches out of his chest next to his carotid artery. I came back from school to find Pokey bloody but unbowed trying to lick the poker out of his chest. When Mom arrived, she took Pokey to Dr Wolfe as the only doctor in the street, although he was an ophthalmologist who had much to do with Mandy in later years. I went with her and, at the front door, Dr Wolfe put his foot on the dog's back and yanked the poker out. "Put Dettol and mercurochrome on it and take him to the vet tomorrow," said Dr Wolfe unconcernedly. Pokey hardly showed any signs of the injury and two days later was chasing the car down Park Street with his rear legs overtaking by his front legs as his claws clicked on the tar. Mom and Dad had to drive fast to shake him off. He returned home with his pink tongue hanging far out of his mouth.

Then there were the white rats. Wayne also wanted to breed them for the Witwatersrand University lab. Judd and I shared a room with two cupboards linked by a curtain pelmet over the window. Wayne installed four rats and a wooden box on the top of one of the cupboards and we threw food up to them, so tall were the cupboards. The rats never climbed down or fell off the cupboards. As we approached with food, their pink noses and whiskers poked over the edge of the cupboard in excited anticipation. The four were soon eight and then, exponentially, the numbers grew so that we were throwing whole cabbages and hardboiled eggs onto the cupboards. We grew accustomed to the scrabbling and squeaking, and we delighted in the multitude that stared down at Judd and me at ritual feeding time.

Then the phone began ringing at odd times. There was never anyone at the other end of the line and Mom had the Post Office come to correct the fault. The linesman first checked the instrument. He then followed the line from the pole in the road. Then he followed the line from the jack through the house to our room and up to the top of the cupboard. With some disgust he got off his ladder and said to Mom: "Meddem. It's your rets." They had chewed off the plastic covering of the wires and every time they peed it short-circuited the line and the phone rang. Wayne had to take what rats he had bred to Wits. That was the end of that programme.

We never had to worry about sartorial elegance. Our wardrobe, even before the time we went to "big school", consisted of khakis. Khaki shirts, khaki shorts and khaki socks. Clark's sandals and rubber soled shoes and, for a bit of colour, Bairnswear pullovers, samples from HE Babb & Son. If we went to a party, it would be in school uniform – or khakis. None of the three lusted after anything else. Khakis were just right for playing war. We had bought steel helmets left over from the desert campaign from ME Military Surplus Stores and our pellet guns were our weapons (not to be fired or pointed at another human). Our next-door neighbour, Caroline Serrurier, was roped in as a nurse. "You're dead!" "No, I'm not – I shot you first." Khakis were just fine for sitting in the zinc tub and being pulled at speed down the bottom lawn. Khakis were suitable for flying kites made of split bamboo from the garden and newspaper stretched over brown string and folded over and pasted down with grey, gooey paper glue. When the August West wind blew, the kite reeled out a whole ball of string and tugged away above the Martins' Norfolk pine. Called to lunch to eat Emily's macaroni cheese on Saturday, I tied the string to the willow tree and left it flying as high as a kite on the fourth of July, but when, after rushing lunch, I got back to the bottom lawn, the kite was hanging upside down with its tail drooping down at the top of the Norfolk pine. And there it stayed because no tugging would free it. Soon it was a skeleton and then the string and tail gave way and the bamboo fell into the tree's branches. That champion kite took two months to die.

Mom and Dad had decided we would go to St John's as the superior school of Joburg. Dad had been at the College. Mom was convinced that this school was the best and that the green blazers of King Edward VII, the blue and white striped Parktown Boys High, the maroon of Houghton School and the light blue of Highlands North would not suit. Besides, they were government schools, and the boys were not "one of us". She so inculcated in us this firmly held belief that nothing could match St Johns in Joburg, that I believed in it. Judd, who had a wider circle of friends from other schools, did not have the same superiority complex. It was only when I went to Lens camp for cadet training that I discovered boys like me from a multitude of other schools and made friends, that it finally dawned on me that I had been duped and that teaching and sports were run on more relaxed and informal terms in other schools. "Yes, but they don't teach Latin," said Mom. And the thought of Catholic schools like Marist Brothers and Christian Brothers were beyond the pale – although they did teach Latin.

What went wrong? Mom clearly thought me bright. I won the Form Prize in Lower I. I won the Maths Prize in Upper I. I won the English Prize in Lower II and then nothing. Nothing till I got to Sixth Form. How did that happen? No need brooding on it. The teachers were like civil servants and there was little panache, little enthusiasm, little spicing-up or real encouragement. Respect, politeness – all male teachers were "Sir", all females Miss Maarschalk, Mrs Rose-Innes. The tunnel of school was enclosed in sports, in physical ability, in smartness. So, I went down a narrowing path that squeezed out from mainstream effort the hobbies and pastimes that engrossed me: stamp-collecting, birds and ornithology, especially at the Birdhaven sewage works. It was I that asked the form-master, JAD Bickmore, if we could not start a bird-club when we were in Upper III and, marvel of marvels, oh joy, oh rapture unforeseen he did, and boarders joined so that they could get out of school to go bird-watching.

Mom and Dad were as much to blame for this dead-end in education. Once they had sent us to St John's, they abdicated all duties in education and trusted the school implicitly to do that. The adult library at home was limited to the Berry and Georgette Heyer books and the Children's Encyclopaedia of Arthur Mee. Since neither parent read widely, they gave no guidance – that was up to the school. Dad was only interested in our sports prowess and there he was satisfied with Wayne's athletic ability: he was tall and could run like the wind. Judd and I were plodders. I got to the second soccer team as goalie but only swimming appealed to Judd and me. As I said, no use brooding on it now, but the narrow view of St John's as the *nec plus ultra* of excellence deprived me of a wider acceptance and curiosity and of taking initiatives in new knowledge. When I rode my bike to the lovely and stately Joburg public library in Sauer Street, the librarians would not allow a person of under 12 to read in the reference library. Oh no, those stern-faced lesbians behind the raised counters in the reference library directed me over their spectacles to the junior library and watched eagle-eyed that I left. In the junior library was the usual dreck in tattered illustrated books. It was dispiriting.

Judd ready for any adventure

Wayne had many good friends of entirely different schools and interests – Jinks Wyllie, the madcap illustrator who gave Wayne a drawing of a man on a barstool: "They said I shouldn't drink and drive so I sold my truck!" Jeremy Borchers went to St Stithians, the new Methodist School, which Mom delighted in calling "St Stickeybums".

For Judd, St John's was toxic, and I blame the boa-constrictor hold on the boy as the primary reason for his suicide. He went through all the motions. But he was happy in his friendships: the Martin twins, who lived opposite and who went to Houghton School, David Potter and Mike Matthews in Trilby Street also in his class, and John Piguet of St Stithians. Illustrative of his easy-going and amicable nature was his enduring friendship with David, or DD, the cerebrally palsied son of the school doctor who was in the same class as he. This bond of boys skated over all the niceties of school and followed its own alternative education. Judd had an IQ of 136, so he knew what he was doing, and he was not doing school. He had already discounted it. He knew this from the way the teachers treated this unconventional boy. He knew a particular woman teacher resented his contempt of her. So, he devised a plan with another boy to write identical essays to be handed in. For the identical essay, the other boy got 80% and "Well done!" and Judd got 40% "Must do better." They showed these to the teacher afterwards much to her blushes, thus ending her prejudice to Judd but not making scholastic life any easier for him. Dad was furious when, at the end of Lower V, the headmaster called him in and said Judd would not be accepted for matric as the school was sure he would fail. This culling was typical of St John's wanting to maintain good matric statistics – no boy had failed for twenty years.

Judd made good in life. I have many long letters from him written to me in Paris and Rome. I am astonished by his erudition, his logic, his *savoir-faire* and his analyses. He often spoke of the martinet teacher, Jack Huggett, and the drunkard, Maxie Burger, whom he held in great contempt. In many ways, I was jealous of his carefree and sunny existence. I was jealous when the art master, Fredericks, brought one of his paintings of show us how a picture could be composed and bold. He worked hard at his swimming, his drumming and his golf. He had an easy-going attitude to everyone and had particularly easy relations with black people – many of his clients became friends and they enjoyed his twitting them and his teasing and light-hearted banter. I was flattered when people stopped in the road and said: "Hey! Judd." We did look alike. He did not resent St John's and took away the respect and politeness that was inculcated into all of us.

* * *

The following chapter is a piece I wrote for the occasion of the 50th anniversary get-together of of our matric class:

Some reflections on St John's

Few families have had five generations at St John's – if any, besides mine. My great uncle was a founding pupil in the corrugated iron hut at the Union Grounds, my father was at the school and boxed there, all three Babb brothers of my generation spent all their schooldays from Lower I at St John's, my son and my nephew and great nephew were sent there. Three Babbs' names are carved in Big School panels for 1st classes.

It is almost with automatic pride in any biographical notes that I include I attended St John's. I am proud of the Herbert Baker buildings, of the attractive badge and of the muted navy blue and maroon colours. The aching question though often worries me – was I educated there?

In this, there are baneful images and reminders which still disturb me. St John's was proud of its musical choral tradition. The man herding

Fancy dress at the Stamps - all sewn by Mom

the school to nasal singing was one Noel Iverson, a short, chain-smoking, asexual and humourless martinet.

Your musical or singing career at the school depended, at eight years' old, on singing together while filing past the maroon-coloured pullover. At this moment, the stick he held pointed you either to the row of benches or the back of the music-room, where I ended. With many others I was surplus to requirements and spent forty minutes a week unhappily standing on the raised back bench for six years. That was the attentive music training I received.

The school is a religious institution and we duly marked "Div" on our timetables for a weekly period. Divinity was presented to us at first by Rev Jarvis Palmer, a tall man who only gained my interest because urban rumour had it that he was involved with the murdered Bubbles Schroeder which had led him to the priesthood.

Try as I might, I cannot remember a single religious, Christian or moral principle, precept or belief that he imparted to us. Oh no, sorry, he taught us the difference between transubstantiation and consubstantiation – the entry of Christ's body into the host at communion, the Roman Catholics (oh, yes, that too – we were all Catholics, but the Vatican was Roman) proclaiming the host becoming the body. At the census he told us not to enter "Anglican" as our religion in the census forms but "Church of the Province of South Africa". One little item he dropped was that there is no letter "V" in Greek so he was Jarbis Palmer

I had to be christened and then be confirmed by the diminutive bishop Reeves, because my parents had left baptism to me to decide on. We went to catechism classes in the crypt chapel which also remain a void in my memory. A dreaded moment arrived when we were fifteen and bidden to Jarvis-Palmer's study above the headmaster's office to be grilled on our teenage sins. My interview went like this: "Do you know about wanking?" "Yes." "All boys do it," he said. I was shown the door.

The short period that Edwin Sulter took divinity with us while Jarvis-Palmer went to Greece, added little to the panoply of religious knowledge

I managed to absorb by myself and by reading. He read us the Screwtape Letters by C. S. Lewis, a wacky bit of reverse psychology involving the devil writing to his son.

From Lower I onwards, we went in crocodile to the chapel for mass on Thursday mornings. The tedium was only relieved by the white mice we kept in our pockets and by passing notes. The religious ensemble of "Div" has led to my being a nominal Anglican and a pagan with deep scepticism about Christianity. If a Christian school treats the belief system so lightly, we have reason to doubt the commitment to being "rightly trained in body mind and character to serve Thee well in Church and State" declared in the school prayer.

The third dominant thread in the weft of St John's lay in sporting performance – not in the fun of participating but in the competition to end amongst the chosen few. If only, if only we had received good advice like: you will never excel in that sport, concentrate on others. But how could this be when the only sport I could master well, swimming, was allotted to Maxie Burger as trainer. The gods must have played a trick on us. On the other hand, imagining Maxie in the sea brings Southern Rights to mind. Until my pocket money ran out, I trained with Ian Colwell at Hillbrow indoor baths, but he was more interested in his Southern Transvaal team than a kid from St John's.

I was witness to Maxie Burger's telling the athletics team: "You boys think I know bugger nothing. You got it wrong. I know bugger all." He was right on both counts. When Malcolm Spence won the 440 yds. at the Commonwealth Games, Maxie Burger said: "I trained that boy." Invited to speak to the school, Malcolm Spence told us he had spent years trying to unlearn the start from the blocks Burger had taught him.

So, like everyone else, I did the tabloid sports, failing the high jump every year, descended from Under 14A over the years to the Second XV.

I played in the cricket league where Teddy Lester (when his wife, June, was pregnant: "June is busting out all over") occasionally made his way to one of the matting creases for the odd sarcastic remark. Our rugby coach

Under 13 was one pasty-faced Harden, an Ulster rugby player who wore the bloody Ulster hand on his faded green rugby jersey.

Maybe I was the only one invited on a Saturday morning for a "physical" in his room in Nash House, eventually stripping down entirely and standing for ages on his scale while he disappeared into his bathroom probably to masturbate, while on his radio the song "We've been invited to Henrietta's wedding, but we don't know when it will be," played. The school hierarchy must have rumbled him because he disappeared from the staff mysteriously.

So it was only post school that I was able to begin to enjoy sport as a communal and friendly exercise, rowing for my college in Oxford, playing rugby for the Exiles in Rome with priests in scrums whom you would not have believed had ever entered a church and, unique amongst my peers, becoming an international cricketer, playing for the first ever Italian cricket side against the Indian Globetrotters (and scoring 11 runs), playing water polo for Oxford, winning the 100 metres freestyle at Stellenbosch and playing for the University's second soccer team. Just happy to have the sweat and companionship.

To contain religion, music and sport in one school community, organisation and discipline loomed like a gloomy omnipresence in the sky. In Upper I, I thought a war-wounded Lewis was the top guy – after all, he lined us up for lunch and poked us with his walking stick and hobbled around on his raised shoe. He did not seem to have any other occupation but to herd us.

The Prep School suffered after headmaster Argyll, under a gimlet-eyed gnome called Manby who had a cruel and vindictive streak to him. He abused the boys he taught with apparent pleasure by stabbing them with his pen and when a question was correctly answered, he accused the answerer of being a toady or a sycophant. When one of his children cut off the tip of a finger in the motor mower on the headmaster's lawn, I felt heaven's revenge on such an unpleasant man.

We escaped Nobbie Clark, the last of the priests to run the school, but had the ex-marine Deane Yates thrust upon us. Most Old Johannians have a soft spot for this childless man. His memory for me is vitiated by a long-running incident where his weakness of character and misjudgement spoil any other of his characteristics. Yes, he amused us in a way by ordering us to "elevate your hose" and adopting Blaikies on his shoes as a trademark, but his naïveté marked the incident I now relate as does his inappropriate approval of the design for the buildings of the horrid school extensions along the ridge.

The incident was one which affected the whole school: a boy, Bowker, was in charge of the armoury for cadets. One day he appears before Yates with one of the silver shooting shields scarred badly with a protractor – someone has vandalised it. Someone must own up. The whole school is kept in for two weeks. No-one owns up because the perpetrator is Bowker himself. My younger brother's class knew that in the Prep the same Bowker had written swear words in one of his exercise books and that class suffered the same fate until a handwriting expert rumbled Bowker – did Bloggs not know this?

Then the building extensions – my mother had been Chairlady of the Ladies Entertainment Committee on the school's 60th Diamond anniversary, which arranged the School Appeal and for a year had exhausted her family and herself in a programme of getting pledges to cover the new building at three huge dinners under tents on the "A" field that she arranged, choreographed and supervised. When she saw what was built with the money, she could have shot herself she was so disappointed, but it was Yates who was suckered into it by Herbert Baker's successors in title and old boys, Fleming Architects. Note: when you see a photo or painting of the school, those extensions are brushed out or excluded.

The other source of authority proceeded from the Housemaster, in my case a sour, longshanks with metatarsal bars on his shoes, Bosh Crowther-Smith. You are meant to be someone if you have a nickname, his coming from a habit of saying "Bosh" to any misconstrued answer. We disrespectfully called him "Clouds of Biff" but so jadedly uninterested was he in the goings-on in Thomson's House, that his sole role turned out to be punishment for those the house prefects sent to him. His sole redeeming feature was his second daughter on whom we could occasionally cast our gaze when she returned from St Mary's to his house in Elm Street.

The school has always boasted of the quality of its teachers. Hmmm. I spent eleven years at the school. I must ponder hard to think of any inspirational teacher who evoked in me fire and enthusiasm. Paul Murray says teachers ought to be "edutainers" – after all, *educare* in Latin means "to lead out" or "bring up". All I really experienced was a faintly dull slog. The greatest inspiration came from "Silent Reading", the true innovative invention of the school.

The Prep School brought us Ann Scruton, known as "Screwbum" whose Afrikaans teaching did not run to listening to radio, music or any real Afrikaans speakers. Her pleasure was sitting in the boys' change room lamenting the fact that some of us wore undervests and expressing horror at wintergreen. Latin started with Hoc Henderson who had a tenuous grip on the subject and left teaching to become a butcher, and then the Latin class was transferred to the abovementioned tyrant, Manby. Maths had at last an adequate grounding with JAD Bickmore, but English teachers like Ian Calder made us write essays on "What I want to be when I grow up" and then said that I should go and play Father Christmas in the fire station when fireman was all I could come up with.

Don't talk about art – that was left to a Canadian (it says it all if you know Canadian art) by the name of Fredericks whose contribution to artistic knowledge was how to blend a sunset in watercolours.

The College should have been the venue for serious academic progress, novelty and identification of pupil talent. But it was not. Take English: through Pisswillie Andrewes, four foot and a tickey high with his waistcoat and eternal love for Kenneth Lawson, also teaching at the school, to Martin-Doyle and Rose: did they ever think to put the lousy Dickens we read in context, to explain the relationship between Keats and Shelley, even give us the lurid background to Roy Campbell's angry verse? It was only post-school curiosity that fleshed all this out rather than the dry words on the page; "I am Ozymandias, King of Kings, Look on my works all ye mighty and despair …" to the post-Napoleon archaeological discoveries in Egypt.

Oh, and Maths: lots of homework, little insight from the bullet-shaped Jumbo Ferrandi onwards. We didn't even know there was a philosophy of maths and that Bertrand Russell had posited a single formula for the world. Wow! That would have been cool to know as a fourteen-year-old. Our class was not even put into the ad maths cycle – indictment on whom? Science was, as we heard in so many of our experiments, tasteless, colourless and odourless. At least we learnt the science vocab: Bunsen burners, bell jars, pipettes. French? We learnt from Popsie le Grand who declared that he could not understand the fuss in the school about chasing a ball that had done no-one any harm.

Popsie gave me one of the greatest poignant moments of my life and suffered the most humiliating experience I have witnessed. He went on the Springbok Radio show "60.000 to Go" – sixty thousand pounds if you got the final questions right after weeks under the question master. His subject was Louis XVI. He got to the final round. All of us were listening. The question was simple – "Where did the revolutionaries catch up with Louis after his escape?" He knew the answer, but did not understand the question. So, instead of walking out with £60.000, he gets a pop-up toaster. The bitterness was evident when he said he could not even use it because he lived in a Yeoville boarding house. This did not impede the cruelty of the St John's boys who for years jeeringly said after any failure at the school: "Give that man a pop-up toaster." It was the end of poor Popsie. Then we got the sumptuously bosomed Yvonne Teague, raunchier, but no come-on in French, more interested in telling us of her (imagined) role in the Resistance. No music, no newspapers, no films – just grammar and the matric short stories and poetry. No spark to Rimbaud, Baudelaire or even Lucky Luke and Asterix.

Which leaves me with Afrikaans and Latin. Few people had time for Boetie de Klerk, but I knew he was a real lover of Afrikaans and he was a scion of the Dopper Kerk de Klerks that produced WA and FW. He lent me Afrikaans novels of the depression Thirties, like *Droogte*, got me reading Trompie, the Afrikaans version of *William and the Outlaws* and was the reason for my going to Stellenbosch University. He was one of the few that gently sought out those who showed their interest in his language.

Everyone knows the condescension and the arrogance of Spike Carter, but he took us to devour things way outside Kennedy's Latin Primer (or "Eatin Primer" as we graffitied it on the cover). I have him to thank that I know something that the compilers of *The Annotated Alice* did not: the White Queen says to Alice: "Jam yesterday, jam tomorrow but never jam today." This relates to the Latin word *iam* meaning "now" but in the sense of "already" or "hence" but not "immediate" (today) which is *nunc* in Latin. And then he gave us the declension of *vis* (power) – vis vis vim vonting vonting vi! For the scansion of dactylic hexameters, he taught us: "Down in a deep, dark hole sat an old cow munching a beanstalk." Ah, yes, now we're talking. *Arma virumque canto*, said Vergil. It was for that that I took Latin as an extra subject to third year at Stellenbosch and had the delight of doing Erasmus in Latin and writing an exegesis on Lucretius' *De Rerum Naturae* and Ovid's odes to love.

Sport, academe, chapel, the choir – and the two other elements to look at: drama and Cadets. Johannesburg descended on St John's to see the Gilbert & Sullivan operettas and, sure, they showed a professionalism unique amongst schools. But being on the Iverson back bench excluded me from the circle of boys singing "Sweet Little Buttercup" and "Tit Willow".

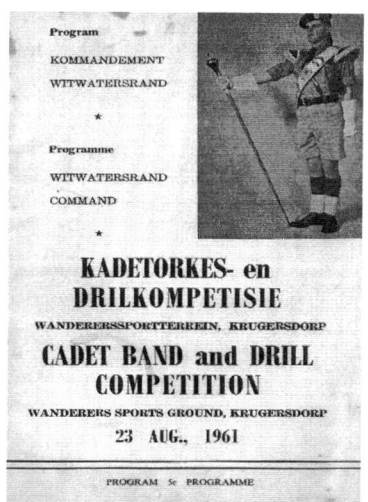

Best Drum Major at Band Competition

Then the bi-annual Shakespeare – the whole school fell in love with Merlyn Sayers as Juliet, but I know of none of my class who became Thespians – nay, Chris Everett sings in all the choirs now, but Iverson relegated him to the same bench as me. Then Martin-Doyle introduced the Grobs, a satirical look at the school and its characters. That was something we could relate to and I embraced it heartily – too late, it came in the matric year – it had the potential to be the Cambridge Footlights – that could have developed a career or two.

The Detachment band seemed to be the only escape from the tedium of marching and wasting a good Tuesday. It also meant you could compete in the Band Competition, one of the few outside competitions the school allowed its pupils to participate in. I took extra trumpet lessons with Hymie Baleson only to find that the pocket money ran out before Hymie's interest in getting his son into a vod (non-Jewish) school and his wasting my precious lesson time in interrogating me about it. Jack Huggett left all the band stuff to the drum major. Before the Band and Drill competition he stood before us with swagger stick under his armpit and yelled: "You will be going to the Band Competition. When you get there, you will be given one white, cardboard box. In it there will be one hard-boiled egg, one sandwich, one apple and one tomato. Guts yourselves because it's all on the Army!" Well, I won the best drum major Stedman trophy, no thanks to Jackie Huggett, but owing to a winter holiday spent at Lens camp under proper tuition from a defence force bandmaster.

So, only two out of thirty odd teachers at the school who taught me led directly to a live interest and expansion into new fields.

An action by the overrated and underperforming headmaster, Deane Yates, summarises the cruelty of St Johns. This action led to brother Judd's later suicide. The chain that leads to that stupid action started back at the link of his Upper V year. Deane Yates called my father in to the school at the end of that year, 1959. In the opinion of Judd's incompetent and colourless, odourless and tasteless teachers, Judd would fail matric the next year. The school could not suffer the humiliation of a matriculation exam failure. Its unblemished record might be tainted, and that could harm the school's reputation. Deane Yates told my father that Judd must repeat the year or leave the school, with heavy emphasis on the latter option. Judd had gone through the same IQ test as I under the watchful eye of Boetie de Klerk and the result was that he had an IQ of 132, almost MENSA level.

Despite his astute and obvious intelligence he went through the prep in the B form and in the college in the C form, his rebelliousness only manifesting itself in the friends he chose and the after school naughtiness like driving the blue Chev lying on the front seat with Davis Potter's Labrador with its paws on the steering wheel, and driving the same Chev down African Street with David Potter and Mike Matthews at maximum speed to get the car to lift off at the dip. Otherwise, he followed the protocols of school. At that time the school had a thing called a "satis card" and the underperformers had to have the teacher initial the card after every class. Judd was issued with this martinet instrument.

Judd's resentment lay deep in his psyche and only towards the end of his life did his disdain for the appalling teaching surface. He also never went to the school after leaving and joining HE Babb & Son. One other profound resentment he confessed to me was not being made Drum Major of the band despite winning the cup for the best drummer and spending a whole July holiday at Lens camp, a cadet camp for all the Witwatersrand schools. The school chose a slab of a witless boy, Rob Wise as Drum Major who had nothing to commend him and only played the tenor drum.

The successes of his life were opening the first Jeans Stores, cut making and trimming for the US BVD underwear giant, opening factories to manufacture Arrow shirts in Hong Kong and Macau, opening the Chloé fashion stores in Rosebank and Port Elizabeth, owning the first Mini GT that he drove till valve bounce and having a 3 handicap at golf. He fell into deep depression when he sold his house at Dainfern and Williams Hunt replaced him for directing their warehouses with the younger Hunt. We could not encourage him to come and stay in Cape Town. His son-in-law, Varrie, called and said they had not heard from Judd for a week – had he spoken to me? Yes, I said, a week ago. Penny went to the cottage (servants' quarters he called it) and the Polish owner told them he had committed suicide and he owed the Pole for a month's rent. Judd had gone to Gilly's house, induced the maid to give him the shotgun and had blown his head off. There his body lay in the police mortuary where it had lain for ten days. The Pole had not thought to let the family know.

The St John's memories that impale one's mind are the quirkinesses and the oddities, not the pure learnedness we saw in the film *The History Boys*. Quirkiness doth not an education make.

Did any of my peer group receive a launch into the ether from their St John's education? They, too, seem to refer more to the bizarre than the inspirational.

I am proud to be an old Johannian. The question remains: Did St John's interrupt my education?

The environs at St John's are nothing less than enchanting, from Long Walk to the Juliet balcony at Darragh Hall. To have spent eleven years amongst them, making up for all the tawdry and stultifying confinements and constraints I experienced, leaves a permanent feeling of peace and wonderment. So, I wrote this little bit of doggerel to compensate for the excoriating review of the school:

#Statuesmuststay – 1949

> When first I saw the David Quad I didn't even think of God,
>
> Though I was standing on his cross of slate –
>
> My eye was drawn to the words and date
>
> Strangely carved half up the tower -
>
> It might have been a little lower:
>
> "First Eleven – Nineteen Thirty" –
>
> When boys enjoyed lost liberty
>
> To play at soccer and even box
>
> And clamber, care-free, on kopje rocks.

My Joburg Family

No time to ponder

Or gape or wander

When Boet de Klerk called me in

To Gate House for that IQ thing,

To ask me to trace a wayward ball

Concealed, he said, by an oval field of tall

Imagined grass and then to number back from twenty.

His approving nod then allowed me in to share serenity

In every quads' own changeless shapes and steady

Forms – Verrocchio's David brooding on Goliath's head,

Pan fluting by the science block,

Della Robbia's angel guarding Mary, and, stock-

Still, the naked boy a-pouring water from a shouldered urn.

But lofty, above the rest, looms the pelican,

Giving its chicks blood pecked from mother's chest.

For eleven summers long I was their guest,

Warmed by them for school's full cycle round.

One soul outlasted me – that's Alf, the carp, in David's pond.

On the statues' plinths: *Ad Majorem Dei Gloriam*, AMDG,

To greater glory of God. I wonder now, you see,

If those still-standing, silent figures in the quads

Give glory to God alone or shelter boys and all their gods?

Back to the family

Children in puberty are confused and rebellious. Judd showed signs of disaffection, but Wayne and I, although restless and pugnacious, conformed to the norms that school and parents imposed. Wayne concentrated on his athletics and his mechanics, I on my stamps and my bugle. The demands of school for sporting excellence consumed most of our waking hours, jogging, kicking a rugby ball and swimming for which I needlessly took extra lessons eating up what pocket money I received at Hillbrow indoor pool with Cecil Colvin and trumpet lessons with the top jazz player, Hymie Baleson. Extra funds were desperately required if you wanted to go the flicks with a girl or get a sports jacket for a bop. I found a solution: waiting. I was seventeen when I started waiting at the Cosmopolitan, a restaurant in Birdhaven.

Joburg was rapidly exiting the city centre – it had started with Rosebank where the first pop-style restaurant, The Pink Poodle, opened. New satellite attractions were emerging in outer suburbs. In the beginnings of Joburg, the City Council allowed corner shops with trading licences to establish themselves in the outskirts and promoters were now exploiting these licences to go further than their first intended purpose, namely, to provide accessible food stores for outlying populations. In Birdhaven, the old man used to frequent a Portuguese market gardener. This licence expanded over his erf to permit the building of a small block of flats and the opening of shops – a hairdresser, the Cosmopolitan and the original Portuguese market gardener. It was to the Cosmopolitan I applied, after swimming at the Wanderers Club's huge swimming pool. The owner was

Alan Dresdner, a funky Jewish entrepreneur. His brother, John, a handsome dentist lothario, lived in the flat above. Alan was pleased to have cheap labour and I was hired at £1 a night plus tips. I could reach Birdhaven by bike. I found the work congenial and even found myself entertaining Alan and John with the fashion of the time, sick jokes: "Mom, Jack's been run over by a steamroller." "Slip him under the door, Sheldon, I'm in the bath." "Dad, how far's Australia?." "Shut up, Sheldon, and keep swimming." So, I was called Sheldon. The tall Mozambican chef used to dance before the stove range. The Cosmopolitan did not have a liquor licence, but wine was served in raffia-bound Chianti bottles and was listed as "grape-juice" on the bill. A pretty girl sat on one of the barstools and strummed folksongs, a group of men got a free meal on Sundays for a half hour of harmonising barber shop quartets. Here I learnt how to make faux cappuccino by stirring white sugar and a drop of water with instant coffee until it was cream coloured and then pouring boiling milk over it. The customers found it delicious and we were never rumbled for not having a cappuccino machine.

It made me giddy to think I could cycle home with £3 in my pocket to use on flicks and taking out the girls. The old folk would only allow me to do waiting once a week and on weekends. The Dresdners took a liking to me and at the end of the evening asked me to tell them more jokes and they doubled up in laughter at this well-bred teenager's straight-faced performance. I gave the staff Christmas presents and the tall chef put his tie on over his chef's jacket and danced on over the steaks and the fried sole. Judd took over from me when I went to Stellenbosch and he was even more popular with them.

When I got my driver's licence in Sixth Form, I could venture for jobs further afield and started at the Bistro, a French restaurant in Parkwood. All about it was meant be genuine French: the tablecloths, napkins and curtains were red and white checked, the waiters wore Lincoln-green long aprons with a pocket and all the crockery was terra cotta. The Bistro operated from a building which had also had the licence for a Portuguese market gardener but had expanded over the whole erf on Jan Smuts Avenue and housed the original market gardener, a hardware, a hairdresser and the Bistro.

The owners of the Bistro were Alekko and Annette Frank, Jews from Alsace who had been dressmakers and branched out into the restaurant business. He was a short plump man with a short temper and she a tall thin middle-aged woman whose top teeth stuck out alarmingly beyond her top lip. Alekko, with Liefie the black cook, stood at the stove while Annette sat on a barstool behind the counter next to a mechanical silver-coloured cash register which *chinged!* convincingly when the keys were pressed and the drawer opened. Both the Franks were true characters, he, surely homosexual and she, at the time I knew her, asexual. The place was popular with the Northern suburb lot attracting the Oppenheimer set. Mary Oppenheimer-Slack-Johnson-Waddell appeared with her noisy, horsey friends and occupied a table for eight, got drunk (if they were not already by time of arrival, usually ten o'clock), and chorused silly, high-pitched falsetto catchwords like "Lovely Ladies" over and over. They were rude, demanding and inconsiderate. I think she was still a bachelorette then because she married my co-student at Oxford, Gordon Waddell, who earned fame by chewing the ear of an opponent in a rugby scrum. Then she married her groom, Bill Johnson, an obstreperous upstart from the wrong side of the tracks in Observatory, Cape Town. His rebelliousness and "up-yours" attitude to the doyen of upper-class South Africa, Harry Oppenheimer, clearly appealed to Mary. When the news broke that they were to marry, Bill Johnson said to the reporter who asked if it was true: "I only ride Oppenheimer horses." Diametrically opposite to Gordon Waddell, Oxford graduate and director of Anglo-American Corporation and Harry Oppenheimer's ideal son-in-law.

Annette was tolerant of all this. At a bachelor party held at the Bistro, for which I was employed as waiter, as the evening got rougher and rougher and more and more plates and glasses broke, Annette calmly sat behind the till, pressing ching-ching! every time something shattered. The best man asked Annette if he could buy the guitar hanging decoratively on the wall and she said: "Yes, if you pay my price." The best man took it down and smashed it over the head of the groom with the strings stretched across his head of hair. A comradely tussle ensued.

As Annette entered the restaurant of an evening, her arms loaded with tubs of meat and heaps of red and white checked napkins, a cigarette-holder clamped between her horizontal teeth, she cried out to the student waiter what was to appear in chalk on the very French slate hanging outside. To my fellow waiter she shouted: "Smoked Scotch Salmon, Two Rands seventy-five." He wiped his hands on his apron and duly went outside to write up the night's special. As the clients arrived, all of them were giggling. As the fourth group came in laughing, Annette went out to see what was causing such hilarity. She discovered the cause on the slate. The student had written precisely what she had said, but transcribed it in accordance with her accent: "Smoked Scotch Semen, R2-75".

It attracted its upper-class clientele because of the very French dishes it prepared, just as South Africans were weaning themselves from mixed grills and chicken-in-the-basket. The winner item was, as described on the menu written in red ink in Annette's very French handwriting: "Half a roast deboned braised duck served with red cabbage cooked in white wine." We sold a multitude every evening.

As we were packing up at the end of one evening and Liefie was shutting down the ovens behind the locked front door and I was placing the chairs upside down on the tables, there came a sharp rap on the glass of the door. Annette, who was sitting reading her most recent, yellow-sleeved Victor and Gollancz book, put down her cigarette-holder and walked suspiciously to the door. We knew that that type of rap meant one of two things: the police checking on sales of liquor or a client who had left something behind. Annette pulled aside the red and white checked curtain over the door with her forefinger and then, in a gesture uniquely rapid in my experience, pressed up the snib of the Yale lock and flung open the door.

On the threshold stood Marlene Dietrich, framed by the door, her hair lacquered away from her cheeks and forehead, wearing a red, sequined full-length dress, high-heel red shoes and long elbow length cream gloves. She tripped in with her slim legs parting the slit in her skirt and looked around bemused as if we should have been waiting for her. Annette frantically gestured to me to take the chairs off the tables. I rapidly set a table for Marlene and the seven leather-jacketed German *Jugenbond* who accompanied her. Mrs Frank handed round the menus and said enthusiastically: "Our speciality is half a deboned braised duck served with red cabbage cooked in white wine", and licked her pencil in anticipation. The seven males all ordered it, but Marlene Dietrich, after reading the menu again, ordered: "Purée of peas cooked with sherry and fresh ground black pepper." You could see the gasp of breath on Mrs Frank's chest. This was the *nec plus ultra* moment of her life. Serving Marlene Dietrich! and she had dismissed the Bistro's *pièce de resistance* so casually. Mrs Frank's knuckles almost dragged on the floor as she walked disconsolately to the kitchen where Alekko was standing anxiously looking on.

The Chianti was poured, and the terra cotta dishes came out, three balanced across my outstretched arms and I carefully placed the purée of peas cooked in sherry and sprinkled with fresh ground pepper in front of Marlene Dietrich. I stood back. Without removing her elbow-length gloves Marlene Dietrich picked up a fork between her left forefinger and thumb and stuck the heft of the fork firmly into the right palm. She could not hold cutlery in her hand. Her arthritis made her hands into claws. She could not cut the duck. She could only lift the purée with a lightly held fork. I quietly walked over to the kitchen entrance where Alekko and Annette Frank, like two little mice, watched out of their hole. I whispered: "She can't use a knife. Her hands are too arthritic." This was a Job's comforter for the Franks who had ached for an event like this in their life only to have a half-triumph.

What compensation when Marlene Dietrich came back again the next night and asked for purée of peas cooked in sherry and sprinkled with fresh ground black pepper.

Marlene Dietrich had appeared at the Colosseum for three nights and a night at the Alhambra in Cape Town because of the determination of Pieter Toerien, who had stood outside her apartment in Paris until he could speak to her and convince her to come and perform in South Africa. He was eighteen years' old at the time. So tickled with Pieter's persistence was she, that she amusedly accepted. I did not know it, but Pieter, who I later got to know well, was among the seven young bucks that had accompanied

Marlene Dietrich that night. He has never looked back as impresario.

I worked at the Bistro in university holidays and also when I was teaching at St John's Prep. The Franks grew to trust me so much that when they went on a month-long European holiday, they handed over the business to me and asked me to stay in their house in Parktown North and look after their three poodles – a standard, a miniature and a toy poodle. This is where I learnt to balance books, make precise orders from suppliers, organise the waiter and cook shifts and even repair broken terra cotta plates. It was with pride that I handed back the Franks the invoices and the receipt book and ledger. They were immensely pleased that the bistro had made a £750 profit in their absence.

Judd followed me also to the Bistro. His personality could not abide the peremptory tone of Annette Frank or the ash drooping off the end of the cigarette holder. In the busiest part of one evening, she shouted at Judd who was serving clients. He took off his apron gave it to Mrs Frank and left. "Where are you going?" she asked desperately. He did not reply, but the restaurant had a giggle at Mrs Frank's discomfiture, he said. He never waited at table again.

At the end of my first year at Stellenbosch University I asked Dad to get me day employment to supplement my waiter's earnings. He obliged by getting me hired as a counterhand at John Orr's department store in Pritchard Street. John Orr's bought much of its foreign clothing through HE Babb & Son. I had known John Orr's only as a customer. My mother, with gloves and hat, frequented the John Orr's tea-room on the third floor where the northern suburbs ladies took tea and scones with whipped cream and strawberry jam. By being a counterhand, I saw the other side of the equation. Getting to the store off the Number 6 bus at half past seven and going round the side into von Brandis Street, I joined employees entering the basement through the staff entrance at which a stern uniformed guard stood. On the first day, I filled in the forms of employment with a group of twenty other students employed for the Christmas holidays and the January sales. The personnel manager gave us each a buff carboard card with our name on it to press into the clock slot to clock in, and, hey presto, the time of your clocking in printed out on the card in the right block. I was filled with jealousy to see the permanent staff swing an arm round a vast disc with concentric holes. The arm had adjustable positions for the pointer which the staff pressed into the hole of their staff number. They did it so easily and nonchalantly. I would have liked to have a staff numbered hole rather than a buff card. The manager said: "Staff must never take the public lifts. Here is the staff lift behind the stairs. Only smoke in the staffroom. Men will always wear a tie and jacket. Girls must wear a white blouse and black skirt. And, I know you students, I've been managing them for twenty years, don't go into the tea-room: only eat in the staff canteen on the fifth floor. Your lunch and tea roster you'll get from the floorwalker." John Orr's employed lift girls who announced at each floor: "Ladies underwear, fashion, shoes and handbags" on opening the expanding trellis door.

The personnel manager assigned us to our departments. The Wits University girls were mostly going to accounts, haberdashery or cosmetics. I went to the men's clothing counter and had to present myself to Mr Engelbrecht, a tall, effete Afrikaner. He was polite but around him there was hubbub. Mr Filmalter was berating Mick McCullum about the shirts out of the cellophane packages. "How can I show customers the shirts without taking them out and taking out the pins?" "Only when you're sure they're going to buy. Look: you've unpacked five! Put them back!" Back and forth this unsolvable argument went. Mr Engelbrecht took me to meet Mrs Pienaar, a dark haired, squat and dull woman who often disappeared to go and gossip with her chums at haberdashery, leaving me in charge of the tie and underwear counter. She taught me how to use the pneumatic tube system that moved cash slips and money to the accounts section. It gave me endless delight to send the slips through the hissing tube in a glass cylinder and to wait for the satisfactory thump of the return of the cylinder with the change.

Then there was a surprise. Mr Engelbrecht introduced me to Attila Káradi, a Hungarian refugee. This acquaintance enlivened the six-week spell of counter-handing at John Orr's. He had been a civil engineer in Budapest and escaped with his daughter and wife across the border to Austria before the Soviet troops arrived in the city in the 1956 uprising. He had looked at the queues outside the embassies of Australia and Canada in Vienna, but the South African queue looked manageable and he opted to apply for refugee status in South Africa. No job had been prepared for him, so wandering the streets of Johannesburg, he saw the name "John Orr's". Orr is a common name in Hungary, so he applied for a job and was given the knitwear counter. His daughter was truly beautiful – a fifteen-year-old at Jeppe Girls' High already speaking proper English. He was so proud of her – she would learn, but he would never rid himself of his heavy Eastern European accent. He taught me some Hungarian: "Hoj von?" How are you? "Hoj von kishlian?" How's your little girl? – a reference to Zsofia, his daughter.

The other counterhands were interesting in having so different a background to me. They spoke with a rough South African accent. I grew to like Mick McCullum who was more or less my age and a bit suspicious and disdainful of the students. He had a zest for life and a sense of humour that the others did not. He also had a Vespa scooter on whose pillion he transported a different girl every day after work. In preparation for the summer sales after Christmas, Mr Engelbrecht sent us to the storerooms under the shop, split up between the various sections by chicken wire. Men's wear neighboured the dusty window-dressing *hokkie*. We were to unload and unpack the shirts and loose collars and studs especially bought in for the sales. Mick spent his time in the window-dressing *hokkie* kissing the lips of the plaster mannequins, caressing them and fooling around and dancing with them. I unpacked the cardboard boxes.

The floorwalker chose our tea and lunch hours. Of course, the students had to be content with hours like 11 o'clock for lunch because the permanent staff, some of whom, like Mrs Pienaar, had worked for three decades for John Orr's, chose the decent hours. The students gathered together at a large table in the staff canteen and were condescending and rude to the permanent staff. They behaved worse with the herd mentality of late teenagers and shouted and teased each other and smoked. I chose not to sit with them. The company of the dull, middle-class sufferers was more congenial especially since my hours coincided with the junior staff.

"What's you name?" "Biscuit" and she giggled to her friend who laughs: "She's Koekie."

I drove to the Káradis who lived in Kensington, which would later be my suburb and which housed the Gem Cinema, barely tolerated by Mom. The hospitality was overwhelming but too deferential. I suppose I wanted to cast my eyes on Zsofia again and I arrived in my newly acquired black Jaguar 3.5 litre 1947 with a sunroof and headlights the size of dinner plates. That was swanky. I said it passed everything on the road except a petrol station.

Having a car and driving was essential for a young man in Joburg. David Paget, who shared with me a love and obsession with the books by Ronald Searle and Geoffrey Willans featuring Nigel Molesworth, *Down with Skool!, How to be Topp* and *Back in the Jug Agane*, and I had seen an Austin 7 standing on blocks at the Kew resort where we had gone to swim and watch the girls. It was a 1932 model open, with what was once a canvas roof, and spoked wheels. From the pattern of sand around the tyres, it had stood aeons where it was, unused. We went to the reception and the owner called his son, a callow youth, not one of us. He looked at us suspiciously, these two bourgeois teenagers. Yes, he would sell it *voetstoots*, as it was. We will have to tow it away and the cost will be £10 cash. We consulted each other and I could afford £7: could David find £3? The next weekend, Wayne brought his spanners and a pump. We bolted on the spoked wheels and pumped up the tyres. The brakes did not work, the callow youth told us, but the handbrake was a cable brake and would stop us from bumping into the towing car. Anxiously we rode behind Wayne in the old folks' new car, a Plymouth station wagon, coloured bile green. We pushed the Austin 7 to a position outside the workshop which housed Wayne's tools and quickly got to work lifting off the body, removing the battered seats and jacking up the now bare chassis and engine and radiator. The bolts were all British Standard Whitworth (BSW) and British Standard Fine (BSF) which had different thread sizes. The Austin seemed to have both so, to start with, we were blindsided when we wanted to put the sump back on with new bolts and found that, although the heads were the same size, the thread was not, so we stripped the female threads on the engine block and had to buy taps and dies to remake the female thread. We got the cylinder head off and there we saw what had caused the car's breakdown; the pistons had a series of thin piston rings that were not the right size and had gouged the block. We bought new piston rings and had the piston rod-ends covered with white lead because they were designed without loose bearings on the big-ends. The copper head gasket was split. Only at Babbage's spares could we find the right-sized piston rings and a head gasket that fitted.

We mounted the engine on the chassis, bought a battery and new spark plugs and put a bit of petrol into the carburettor. The moment of truth arrived. We had no electrical knowledge, so the starter motor had not been reinstalled. At the first turn of the crank-handle the little one-litre engine sprang to life with a roar undampened by an exhaust pipe or a silencer. Children rushed up from all over the suburb and gawped at this miracle. I could have hugged myself as I turned off the ignition. When I had attached the exhaust and silencer, I placed a wooden Schweppes box on the chassis and sat behind the steering wheel. Without a floor, I could not fix on the

Jag passes everything on the road except a petrol station

David Paget's and my 1932 Austin 7

brake and accelerator pedals, though the clutch pedal was attached to the gear box. For the accelerator, I tied a length of string to the carburettor lever to hold and pull next to the steering wheel and I trusted the handbrake to stop the car. Off we went down the drive sitting on the Schweppes box and pulling on the carburettor string to set the car in motion. For a few days, we drove the car round the block, along Park Street, down Stella Street, along Meyer Street and back up African Street. There was little traffic in Oaklands, but a busybody did stop me and order me to take "this wreck off the road."

One incident ensured that we quickly put the body back on. Judd was given the chance to ride the Austin. He sat on the Schweppes box and, unwisely, tied the accelerator string to his forefinger. As he took off down the drive, the steering wheel came away from the steering column. The nut that held it on was too large for our spanner set and had only been screwed on finger-tight. The Schweppes box fell backwards with Judd's finger still tied to the accelerator which opened with alacrity. The car took off at speed down the drive with Judd lying prostrate on the chassis and the accelerator fully open. Helplessly, I ran after the chassis as it tilted down the drive and across Park Street to crash into the Martins' gate. My first thought concerned the radiator which had taken the main impact and only then Judd, who was unconcernedly still lying on his back with a smile on his face. "That was exciting," he said, shook himself erect to examine the damage. Apart from some bent flanges on the radiator, there was none. The car had stalled, but one turn of the crank-handle, and it came alive again and we could put the steering wheel back on its splines and return to the workshop. A large spanner to fit the nut and the return of the body to the chassis were now essential.

The Austin 7 was popular because it was cheap and the design was cheap – cable brakes, cable clutch, rudimentary shock absorbers and, worst of all, the whole car's propulsion depended on two half-moon washers, snugly fitted into semi-circular cavities in the left and right axles. These washers had to take the whole weight and motion of the car and broke continually, an eccentric British design fault. A friend who had owned an Austin 7, Theo van Schaik, told me that if he went anywhere in the Austin, he took a pocket full of half-moon washers with him. This proved to be the end of the road for the Austin. In our case, the half-moon washer on the right axle broke the axle. We no longer had the patience to rummage through the second-hand car parts lots or visit the firm of Babbage's Spares to find an axle for a 38-year-old car. We had never been able to work out the electric circuit for the generator or the starter motor, so we decided to sell and placed a smalls ad in *The Star* under "vintage cars" and soon were able to hand it over for £25 to a wealthier enthusiast. I was going to Stellenbosch University and David was heading for England to go to the bar and where he became judge in the English High Court of Justice.

My permanent place in Joburg was now coming to an end. I was to live in three different suburbs in Johannesburg after Stellenbosch and the diaspora from 17 Park Street was beginning. The old folks moved from there with Mandy five years later. Wayne had gone to Port Elizabeth. Judd stayed with his wife Judy for a while in the converted garage and then moved first to Norwood, and with his business growing, to Sandhurst. Wayne moved back to Walkerville, and I left to live in England, so the only constant permanent anchor for Joburg after my parents' death was Judd. Since this narrative centres on my Joburg family, what I shall write from here on will relate to our family members' links to Joburg as we come and go, leave and return, abandon and find our connection to it again. It is like a moth that circles the flame – our coupling with Johannesburg has never died and Judd's offspring make this association durable – never-ending to such an extent that one of Judd's daughters, Jossie, bought the house next door to 17 Park Street, then owned by Mrs Hickman.

First me: after I had graduated at Stellenbosch, St John's Prep School offered me a teaching post in Latin and Maths because one of their teachers, Michael Quail, had developed narcolepsy, a disease that always makes you drowsy and sleepy and Quail had fallen asleep often in class. The symptoms can be alleviated, but there is no cure. He had asked for leave for treatment and the period allowed was nine months which matched the time between my leaving Stellenbosch and going up to Oxford, so. I would go back to Joburg. The school was desperate and took me on even without any teaching experience. Of my Latin, I was sure; of the Maths, not so much. Anyway, I would only teach in Upper II and Lower III for R75 per month. The school assigned me a small bedroom and, across the corridor, an office adjoining the boarding house. I had to supervise morning showers and evening homework for the boys. This suited me fine: I could work some evenings at the Bistro and study for the distance learning Ll.B course at the University of South Africa, for which I had enrolled.

I can, in all honesty, say the Prep boys taught me more than I taught them. Each day was a revelation. There were two other masters who began at the same time as I – Jimmy Weinbren and Terence Hall. Jim was an adopted child who had grown up in Joburg and taught art. He drew fine line drawings and had been to Wits University under the tutelage of Cecily Sash, who emphasised drawing in all her teaching. He took over the arts teaching in the Prep. He was allotted the flat above the cricket storeroom on the "A" cricket field with his wife. When we found we were worshippers of The Goons, our friendship was sealed for ever. We used address each other "Nickle nackle nidle noo"; what is that ringing? Must be the phone, Min." Terence was a fine sportsman and besides teaching English took on the sports duties except for swimming. The chance to be in the staffroom and to be called "sir" tickled me immensely. With two teachers more or less my age, the staff tea was relaxed and the staff meetings under the headmaster, Paterson, unthreatening. The Afrikaans mistress, Trixie Palmer, took me under wing, invited me to supper at home, and after a visit with her husband to the Bistro, laughed and said she would not split on me to the school for working two jobs.

Because of my young age, the relationship with the boys was relaxed and avuncular. I told the boarders horror stories at bedtime like "Sweeney Todd, the Barber", until, one day, a boarder called Davies, came into my office at about nine. "I can't sleep, sir," he said. The stories I told after that catered to the more sensitive boys. But I could be goalkeeper in their informal soccer matches and teach them how to make kites with the bamboo below the Valley field and make *woer-woers*. I was at ease with them and with myself. When, after nine months, I left, I got letters from some that I taught, like

Robert Sneesby, who, to make things more difficult, could not pronounce his "s's" which came out in a sort of nasal snort. He wrote:

28 Talbragar Ave
Craighall, Johannesburg

Dear Mr Babb,

It is R. Sneesby writing.

There are some new students and a woman the woman has received valentine cards from Linder and one from Niven, who is know a monetor, so is Cotteral who is captain of cricket ...

It was like reading out of *Down with Skool* and Nigel Molesworth.

21/11/65

Dear Mr Babb,

Thank you so much for the postcard you sent me. Please come back and teach us history because Mr Quail is boring and does not act it like you did... Lincoln College does not look a bad place from the postcard. Mr Quail said it was not good at sport but it has brains...

From Ewan King

24th October 1965

Dear Glen,

I got your letter and thought it very thoughtful of you to think of me. Mr Quail is rivising all our Latin ... I hope you enjoyed trip to Italy and the Pope didn't bore you too much. I hope you liked the pen we gave you, we were going to buy you a camera but Mr Wienbren told us you didn't use the one you had very much. The class and I miss you very much after what you did for us, but I am sure you will be a very trustworthy and good loya (sorry if I don't spel to well.) ... I hope you visit Greece I am sure you will like it there. I will give you a ticket to visit Zeus ... Ding, ding, ding, ding. Oh it is time to go to the san. Good bye and good luck,

George Taliadoros"

Back to the family

* * *

Of one thing I am proud and that is the esteem I gave to the rebellious and marginalised. One was a boy called Espley-Jones about whom I was warned by one of the anally-retentive women teachers. He was certainly a hyperactive and robust boy, selfish and self-centred and could be disruptive. He was a dayboy. I imagined there was some dysfunctionality in his home and it turned out this was so. I used to keep him in after lessons and then taught him to play chess on the master's table. It could have been anything, but he craved attention and the narrow female teachers he had had could not cope with his rambunctiousness. After giving him this attention, he did not want to go home. He calmed down. He became helpful and although he tried to monopolise my attention, I ensured he shared time with me with other boys. During the Easter holidays, he asked me to come to his house on Empire Road, Parktown, and meet his parents. The house was precisely opposite Owl Road leading to the Rand Easter Showgrounds and the show was in full swing when I visited. The boy had turned his parents' garden into a parking ground and was charging twenty-five cents for entrance. I shook my head: this boy will go far. I met his father who showed the same boisterous and bouncy Tigger-like characteristics of the boy. His mother was a sweet, submissive person who was bossed around even by her son and his elder sister – all loud and rough.

I have often thought of how I could have done a much better job of teaching. The Latin classes were a breeze and, for two boys, MacKay and Townsend, who came late to the school and had not had Latin, I gave extra lessons at 75c a shot. I found boys who were competent were wanting to come and join the extra lessons. No persuading would stop them, so I had 8 x 75c twice a week. I was rolling in money. The maths class for 10-year-olds could have been a lot more imaginative, but the school had crammed Upper IIB with 30 boys. Good income for the school, but no accountants will emanate from that class, I think. I should just have given them 12 matchsticks and plasticine and they would have understood the idea of units, division and multiplication rather than learning the boring old tables which we recited repetitively every morning.

I do not berate myself too much – sometimes the layman is better than the professional. Iain Paterson wrote to me:

"24th September 1965
From the Headmaster Tel. No. 43-4020

Dear Glen,

I would like to add to the few words I said at the Staff Meeting yesterday.

For a young man with no real teaching experience you have done a remarkable job during the past three terms. Your contribution to the School has been very real and positive. Thank you very much indeed.

May I take this opportunity to wish you every success in the future.

Yours sincerely,

Iain Paterson."

So not too shabby, then. Could have done better, though.

I missed David Paget and our love for the Molesworth books of Willans and Searle from which we quoted *verbatim*: "Skool piano hav never been the same since Molesworth 2 pla fairy bells on it."

As a sort of rebellion against the coven of pronunciation and proper English both our parents exacted we worked on a South African slang dictionary. Here are some of the more tempting words and phrases we eked out of our compatriots:

Don't cock me a rolling donut (lie)

Laid him level with the gravel (knocked out)

Go for a goof (swim)

The Greek/caif/caffy (café)

Kyk my skeef   (askance)

Squeeze your lemon (pee)

Noombies (breasts)

Jive on my liver

Cream your jeans (ecstatic)

Jol (party)

Don't tune me grief

Gooi a greenie (spit)

Underrammies (underpants).

The dictionary reached 200 entries, but we left childish things on our way to higher education.

During my time at Stellenbosch, I had fallen deeply in love with Ann Skilton, whom I had met at The Cosmopolitan while waiting at table there. I invested heavily in her. Judd said she was very sexually attractive, and so it proved. She was also a Joburg girl – her father, Walter, was a civil engineer with Murray and Roberts, the construction company. He was English and had spent the war as a sapper placing mines and organising defence, like placing bombs under strategic bridges the German invaders might use. He said the only way to keep the explosives dry was to wrap them in contraceptives. He was building the Carlton Centre as chief civil engineer for Murray & Roberts. It was to be the tallest building in Africa. His wife was tiny and was amused by everything with a ready laugh and a quick quip for every eventuality. Her repartee was infectious. Because of her chimney-like smoking, we came to call her Nicotine Nan. Her real name was Audrey and her very Scottish mother worked as a nanny with a Jewish family in Saxonwold and was much appreciated for her dour and dedicated service to their children whom she kept in disciplined control while the parents were occupied with the Jewish social round. She used words like "as skinny as a *tattybogle* (scarecrow)" and phrases like "yoor e'es are bigger na ya belly."

* * *

Ann Skilton in *The South African Tatler*

***Birdie* by Marin**

Joys and sorrows

Ann was struggling with her Latin for matric which she was doing at a cram college, Damelin, after leaving Parktown Girls' High, so I sat with her at her parents' dining room table and give her extra lessons. The Skiltons lived on Upper Park Drive, Forest Town where Werner, Beit & Co had planted the million jacarandas, opposite the Joburg zoo. Ann could honestly tell her circle of acquaintances later in Oxford and also the Oxford city librarian that, at night, from her bedroom she could hear lions roar.

Murray & Roberts had arranged a nightwatchman at their house. He was a Zulu who hummed and chanted rather disturbingly, but later comfortingly, as he patrolled round the house when he was not warming his hands over a traditional brazier which burnt continuously at the side of the house. Ann matriculated and went to the BG Alexander nurses college in Hillbrow and she worked as a student nurse at Joburg General in Hospital Hill while I was at Stellenbosch. Her character did not suit nursing at all with its disciplines and exactitude. She had all the sympathy and caring of a nurse, so much so that a grateful Portuguese couple offered her a bun with a Portuguese recipe frog in it. She did teach me how to inject someone's bottom – top outside quarter so you did not paralyse your patient, and she practised on an orange. She abandoned the career after six months and was employed as librarian by the Joburg City Council. I was too blinded by my attraction to her not to see how she could not cope with time restraints, application and determination. She was later diagnosed as being severely depressive. What did I know about depression? In our Joburg family you pulled up your socks, faced problems and did not wilt. Never did it come to mind that you could not manage, whatever the obstacles. The signs were too apparent and as I entered the diplomatic corps, the demands on her simply overwhelmed her.

Another aspect of depression involves inappropriate behaviour to escape the obligations and duties of normal life. The depressive feels a void and fills it with a high, a type of drug. A depressive is also less committed to a relationship and uses escape hatches. In her behaviour, I should have been warned that infidelity would ensue, but I blundered forward, certain that we could together face the slings and arrows of outrageous fortune and immersed myself in her. I wrote her a letter almost daily and maybe got one reply in ten, but I was so happy to see her when I got back to Joburg. "I wrote to you so often, but I threw the letters away – they can't compare with yours," and I believed this tale. She worked at the Rosebank library in Joburg and, in my holidays, I picked her up and took her home in my MG TD which Wayne had passed on to me on condition that I got it roadworthied and licensed. Not an easy task, but I heard that Primrose roadworthy centre near Germiston was less strict, so I got a mechanic to take it there and, for a bottle of whisky and repairs to the suspension and the brakes, I had my roadworthy.

I bought a 0.6 carat diamond ring which she later negligently lost in Ireland and we were engaged which made me very happy, but Ann seemed to take it rather indifferently. Her engagement photo appeared in the *Tatler* at Mom's insistence, and Mom did her best to make Ann at home at our always noisy table, though she never got into a bathing suit with us because she wore an old-fashioned corset. Judd's relaxed and teasing nature relaxed her and they both chatted unconcernedly. Ann had broken her front tooth in a dive in a swimming pool in Welkom and Wally, her father, had seen good to have it filled with gold. This blemish in her appearance I tried to convince her to correct and I took her to Squibbs Kark, the family dentist, but she phoned me in my office in Pretoria from the dental chair saying she could not go through with it. Squibbs took the receiver: "Never mind. The Europeans like gold teeth and she'll do fine in France," which was to be my first foreign posting.

After my teaching stint at St John's Prep, I left for Oxford, accompanied

Joys and sorrows

by Mom with a stopover in Italy, arriving in Rome at five in the morning and I had my first jaw-dropping experience of Mediterranean life – men in string vest hanging up washing on balconies, wheelbarrows full of tomatoes and tiny Fiat 500's winding amongst the traffic. Deciphering the Latin inscriptions on the monuments. Walking through the Borghese gardens that very morning to the Etruscan Museum opposite the Modern Art Museum. I thanked Spike Carter and Prof Hugo for their Latinate groundwork.

Since this is a Joburg story, I shall mention only the returns to the Joburg hub from the spokes along which we children had spread out to the perimeter. I left to start the Michaelmas term from October to December, the term named after St Michael whose saint's day is 29 September. (The other terms were Hilary after St Hilary, saint's day 14 January and Trinity eight weeks after Easter the theological origins of Oxford lasting through to this secular age.) Ann joined me a couple of months later in Oxford where she worked in the city library, but Joburg called again when we returned to marry on 30 April 1966.

We returned by BOAC and were delayed in Nairobi, so I could not marry with banns, but had to apply for a special licence at the Department of the Interior. We rushed the arrangements because we had only three weeks to put the invitations, the ceremony, clothes hire and the reception together. The reason for the rush was that Ann was pregnant. Neither of us told our parents, wanting to spare them the blushes, and acting "normally". We had been engaged for two years. I do not doubt they had their suspicions, but these were never expressed. The charade covered the uncertainty and the invitations calling me Glenn Robin Hare Babb made me spring to it. I stayed at 17 Park Street and Ann with her parents in Forest Town.

The St John's College chaplain, Rev Sulter, agreed to conduct the ceremony at St Michael's Church in Bryanston. Wally and Nicotine Nan arranged to hold the reception at the house of one of Wally Skilton's directors at Murray & Roberts, Fred Law, in Bryanston. Our flight back was booked for the very evening of the wedding.

Wayne and Judd were much amused by this haste. Judd was my best man. We looked spiffing in our morning jackets. I had bought Ann's wedding gown in Bond Street at John Lewis with money earned waiting at the Cherwell Boathouse restaurant on the Cherwell River in Oxford. I waited for Ann at the altar at 11 o'clock and she came in with her bridesmaid, Annemarie Willcox, who later became a protective masquerade for Ann, running interference in the American football way.

Ann's train was long and carried by Annemarie. I clumsily stood on it until Sulter slapped me angrily on the shin. When we knelt to take our vows, a titter ran round the congregation. Wayne and Judd had painted in white Shu-Shine on the instep of my shoes: "HE-LP".

In the late autumn sun, we sat at tables on the Laws' lawn and ate the wedding breakfast, Judd, in his morning suit, playing master of ceremonies and gently teasing his university brother and the Joburg élite. Of course, Annemarie caught the bouquet and Judd the garter. He was later to be best man at my wedding to Tracey.

The day of the wedding was a portent of what was to come for the next 17 years. No urging, no encouragement, no inducement would make Ann

"HELP" on the soles

hasten her packing. She had to phone her brother, Clive, in South West Africa, a long-distance call which required the intervention of a switchboard and he was nowhere to be found. She cried and would not leave until the call was made. A long conversation followed. Pure prevarication. Kicking for touch. In her soul she did not want to go back to England.

The next year, 1967, both Wayne and Judd got married. There was dissent as to who would have first dibs. Janet, Wayne's fiancée and Judy, Judd's, were not on speaking terms in their contest to be the first. Separated by a couple of weeks, Wayne went first. He married Janet Hooper, the daughter of the former private secretary of Prime Minister, Jan Smuts, Kenneth Hooper. There was never an opportunity for me to ask about his experiences. Judd married Judy Todd, who also lived in Park Street, the daughter of a geologist and gemmologist, who had the patience of Job and had helped Mandy with her maths homework when she was getting 16% for her tests.

Judd had made the best of his school-leaving and had cleverly got the agency for Lee Jeans – sure, it was not Levi's, but jeans had become so popular in the hippy and flower-child era, that imported jeans caused queues outside the shops he opened, called simply "The Jean Store". He had three branches, rather amateurish, with no shopfitting which had its own downside when a girl was pushed against the full-length mirror leaning against the wall. The mirror broke and the top half slid down cutting into the girl's calf. Shortly after this, Judd's Jewish partner slyly arranged for the fire alarm to go off one night and for the water nozzles to spray all over the merchandise, much to the distress and chagrin of Judd. The insurance pay out allowed him to make a belt with small gold bars in its pouches and to flee to Los Angeles, never to be heard of again. Judd continued with the stores in town, Rosebank and Port Elizabeth, where one of the Martin twins, Graeme, our former neighbour lived after doing his military service in the Navy.

His anger and frustration at having had to leave St John's, where he would undoubtedly have been the next Drum Major, was now appeased and he was innovating at HE Babb & Son in a way Dad would never have thought of: he started a cut, make and trim business with John Piguet for BVD, the colossal US underwear manufacturer, and, before long was able to move out of the rented accommodation in The Village and had bought a morgen property in Sandhurst with a lawn as big as 17 Park Street stretching down to swimming pool with Alsatian dogs, later to be joined by a macaw.

Our next trek to Johannesburg came when we returned from Oxford on the Union Castle Line Cape Town Castle, all painted lilac and on its way to India via Cape Town to be cut up into scrap. The legend is that you can walk on the seabed from Cape Town to Southampton on silverware thrown out of the portholes by lazy stewards. I was returning with an eight-month-old baby, St John, named after one of my best friends at Oxford, St John Crabtree. The English pronunciation gives pause as it sounds like Sinjin. When he was about to marry, his future mother-in-law asked nervously if Jen was marrying an Indian? Also, on the ship, along with baggage "Not Wanted on Board" was a 1958 Austin London taxi in which we had criss-crossed England. It cost me £75 and was the last three-door design. The space next to the driver was a platform for luggage. In London, a taxi-driver could not re-licence a taxi older than ten years, so whole businesses existed to dispose of them.

**Penny, Jossie and Robyn Babb at Judd's pool
- never have an Alsatian, it bit Robyn**

Joys and sorrows

I saw the ad in *Exchange & Mart* and went up to London to meet a spiv-looking, stove-pipe trousered, greasy man wearing winkle-picker shoes. For ten pounds extra he would give me a taximeter ("but don't use it for clients, the bobbies will arrest you.") This car was to be my runabout till I left for my first posting in Paris for the Department of Foreign Affairs.

The licensing of taxi cabs in London falls under the 1843 Hansom Cab Act whose provisions applied to horse-drawn cabriolets and, later, merely extended to motorised vehicles. So, a cab has to be able to turn around the circle in front of the Savoy Hotel without reversing. Gulbenkian, the richest man on the planet, found the vehicle so congenial that he bought one for his own personal use. He is reputed to have said: "It can turn on a sixpence, whatever that is." It must be tall enough for a man wearing a top hat to sit comfortably in the rear seat. It must carry a bale of hay in the boot for the horses, a little provision that the coppers use to arrest and take to the police station, drivers suspected of drug-dealing or procuring. "Will you open your boot, sir, I should like to see if you are compliant with the law and bear a bale of hay?" It was vast inside, had two flap-down seats and plenty of room to stretch out, and you were safe from prying eyes because the Hansom Cab Act did not allow the driver to have an internal rear-view mirror. We drove this diesel monster to Johannesburg with Mandy, St John and Ann in the back and I could slide the window closed so I could be completely separated from baby cries.

Mom and Dad and Mandy had come down from Joburg to meet us. As the tugboat brought the huge liner alongside the pier, we could see the threesome on the dock. Ann collapsed handing St John to me. She sobbed: "Mandy can't see us." She was distraught. One of the English passengers said, concernedly; "Are you alright, dear?" She was not. In our time in England, Mandy's eyes had deteriorated badly and her eyesight was now only partial. More about that in the next chapter on Mandy.

She was still a *bok* for anything. We bundled her into the taxi and set off for Joburg luggage on the luggage platform, in the back and in the boot. Mandy got amusement from anything. Anything. The taxi had a flat tyre outside Beaufort West and the spare was taken out from under a mound of

A large crowd gathered r[...] this London taxi after it [...] discharged from the Capet[...] Castle yesterday.

London cab rouses quayside nostalgia

Cape Times Reporter

MR. G. R. W. BABB returned to South Africa yesterday after two years' studying law at Oxford—and with him he brought a black, high-roofed London taxi.

Nostalgic ex-Londoners clambered in and out of the taxi and toyed with its meter on the quay next to the Capetown Castle.

A Railway police sergeant swore the taxi was Egyptian. "I saw one just like it up north during the war," he explained to the large crowd which gathered around the cab.

And Cape Town taxi drivers clustered nearby in whispered discussion about the vehicle. They were scornful of it and claimed it was ugly.

Mr. Babb, who intends entering the diplomatic service, will use the taxi as his family car in Johannesburg.

"We bought it more as an item of amusement than anything else. In the three months that we've had it we've used it quite a bit," he said.

Mrs. Babb, who had her nine-month-old son on her arm, was enthusiastic. "I think it will be great fun driving round Johannesburg in a London taxi."

baggage. Hardly had it been put on when it collapsed within a mile. I now had to hitch-hike into Beaufort West with the tyre I had removed. Wrong decision. The rim of the tyre had cracked and allowed the inner tube to rub against the wheel and burst, so I took the wrong tyre with me. The tyre was irreparable and the garage did not have the same size and nor did any other garage the manager phoned in Beaufort West so I had to hitch-hike back to the Taxi and fetch the wheel I had just put on the axle. We spent the night in an hotel. It was bad augury when the receptionist pulled out a tube to speak through. He had damaged his vocal cords and addressed us through this device placed next to a hole in his throat. We all slept on beds whose mattresses were filled with mealie-cobs which made Mandy laugh. We were tired enough not to care and had a *plat du jour* in the dining room of stringy Karoo lamb.

In Joburg, we stayed at Wally Skilton's ranch in Douglasdale, a new development in the outward northern spread of Joburg near Fourways. That is the way to name a place – Fourways, like Soggott's Corner, or the Sewage Farm, or Halfway House, or Hospital Hill, or The Fort the reference is clear and embedded in the cultural history of the place. I built a cot for St John, who was already called Squash in the tradition of giving everyone nicknames, out of a sheet of asbestos, four 4x4's and dowel sticks. In my clumsiness, the space between the dowels was large enough for Squash to clamber through, so the effect was spoiled by the string woven between the dowels to prevent his falling out.

We were staying in Douglasdale in anticipation of my interview with the Department of External Affairs at the Union Buildings in Pretoria. When I succeeded after facing a barrage of five Deputy Secretaries, we planned for leaving Joburg for Pretoria. In the new year 1967, the little family moved to *Las Palmas*, a new block of flats in Troye Street in Sunnyside and my short-lived Pretoria experience started. Pretoria, a city of Volkswagens and Alsatian dogs, from which we escaped on weekends under the overarching gum trees on the old Pretoria Road past Grand Central airport, on to Louis Botha Avenue, through Norwood and to the comfort of 17 Park Street. Both Wayne and Judd now had houses in Norwood, the Village, not far from the family hub and so, the family, with new babies, gathered around the old swimming pool, a mass of rambunctious boys again with their new wards and less new wives – Judd with Jilly and, later, Penny, Wayne with Brendan and me with Squash and, later, Bridget (nicknamed Bridie Briddle) conceived on the Cape Town Castle but born by caesarean section in Pretoria, an experience which Ann never wanted to repeat, and did not, becoming a fanatic of the new invention, the Pill. And Mandy, teased and tickled.

Joburg was the flame for my moth after this brief sojourn in the capital. I delighted in knowing that the State would subsidise your mortgage bond even if your house was a distance from your place of work. On return from my posting in Paris, I bought a house at 34 First Avenue East, Parktown North, affordable at R35.000 and not far where we had our early swimming lessons buoyed by cloth water wings tied around our chests at Mrs Clark's. When we needed shoes, Mom took us to a shoe shop nearby in Lower Rosebank which boasted an X-ray machine to check how they fitted your feet. Wonderment to see through the green screen the bones of your feet against the leather covering.

I owned two houses in Joburg after that – one in Kensington opposite the iffy Gem cinema at 6 Roberts Avenue, and then, posh, No 4 St Andrew Road, in Houghton. Kensington's roads east-west are named after the two British Boer War commanders, Roberts and Kitchener and the north-

Kensington 6 Roberts Ave all tarted up

south roads alphabetically after British battleships: Albemarle, Blenheim, Collingwood, Doris, Empress right down to Royal Oak. I bought my house in Kensington on Deed of Sale, so payments were delayed until I could obtain a bond. It was a dark muddy-brown face-brick house built as the Boer War was ending. Typical of the colonial villa style, a stoep ran round the front and side, pressed steel ceilings soared tall over the spacious rooms. The garden was handkerchief sized but I paved the back yard where I could dine in the soft evening warmth of the Highveld.

At the Kensington house, always scraping pennies together after leaving Ann, I taught myself bricklaying, I roofed the spare room with new corrugated iron, I built steps down from the garage roof into the side garden, I tiled the bathroom and the kitchen, I put up new beams in the gables, I wallpapered the dining room, repaired the chimney and mantelpieces in bedroom, dining room and sitting room, and I built a front wall at the roadside. As I stood sweating with dagga on my trowel, a local paused and stood admiring my workmanship: "It's coming on, the cabin, eh," he said to my great satisfaction.

The side garden had been the storage place for coal and everything grew there, fertilised by the coaldust and the apricot tree was prolific. Standing on the flat garage roof, the full beauty of a Highveld sunset spread over the house from the west. It lent itself to a deckchair and a glass of cold gin and tonic leading to amusement and the jealousy of the passengers on the upper deck of the No. 24 bus going into Joburg who sometimes cheered through the bus's windows at such decadent leisure.

A fundamental error occurred when I decided to paint the whole house a deep Icelandic red. In the beginning, it really looked sharp, but with the Highveld sun's rays, the red took on a maroon and then brown hue.

Each day I commuted to Pretoria in my left-hand drive Beetle, loading up two colleagues to share costs. I was head of the West, North and Central Africa division and was leading a campaign into Africa. This house hosted, as overnight guests, Idi Nadhoim, Vice President of the Comores, René Duval, Minister of Foreign Affairs of Mauritius and Gaetan Duval's brother, Bula

Nyati, Prime Minister of Zaïre and Hassan Wehelie, a confidant of President Siad Barre over whose kneeling body I almost fell while he was saying his evening prayers, who brought South Africa to the negotiating table with the president and who was the first black person to co-host a political party meeting with a Nat in my Randburg parliamentary campaign where he sat on the platform with me. Judd ensured that his daughters were accepted at Kingsmead College.

This house to which I dedicated so much love and attention, which was my personal creation and had such authentic colonial charm, even with a coal AGA stove, was not to the liking of my next wife, Brenda Bedborough, mostly because of the area in which it was which she did not feel comfortable inviting her friends to visit. I was delighted to have people round and received all with pride for the character of the domicile. I moved reluctantly to Houghton, *the* suburb after Parktown and Westcliff. The Kensington house appealed to the gay community, so my first tenants were all keen on ripping off the staid wallpaper I had hung so laboriously. The subsequent tenants, after the house had been neglected were non-swimmers and soon rent was not being paid. When I came up from Cape Town after my return from Rome to inspect my "cabin", the bath had been

Bridie and Squash at Kensington

taken out, the geyser had been sold, the mantelpieces I had lovingly restored were gone, the carpets had been ripped out, the gas stove had been sold and the loo was now a large bucket in the sitting room. The garage had become a spaza shop. A colony of rats had installed themselves under the kitchen floor and had burrowed a nest in the accumulated rubbish pile in the elegant backyard. I bought two boxes of Rattex and spread it wide and at the mouths of the dens.

Judd, at the time, had opened a golf driving range and had tough workers fetching the balls and watering the green. I hired his squad with big sticks and took them to 6 Roberts Avenue. Within half an hour they had driven out the ten *skollies* with their meagre belongings. The tenant to whom the house had been let had the temerity to ask if they could not stay on, and the spaza shop lady pleaded that she continue her business. No. Out. And as soon as they were, Petrus Mogaba and his gang of stick-wielders helped me shovel out the rubbish accumulated over four years into a skip I had hired. This was soon too full. I looked at my ruin and mourned. I did not have the courage or the patience to start all over again, so I sold it to the new owner of the Gem Cinema making much of the still intact air vents in every room made to look like little trunks of trees, the pressed-steel ceilings which had survived this barbaric onslaught, the stained-glass window Bridie and I had made for the front door and the Oregon pine floors. A smidgeon of its character remained, and this was enough for the buyer to fork out R100.000.

Houghton. It certainly had cachet. After all, Mandela himself went to live there. Helen Suzman, now not the only Progressive Party Member of Parliament, was still its representative in Parliament. It housed St John's College and the Houghton Golf Course. The Wilds was still *the* place to have your wedding photos taken. Jacarandas still lined the streets and oaks up on the streets named after Saints. I bought a double-storey at number 4, St Andrew Rd. The management of St John's used to get cross when the roads were apostrophised – they would peevishly say: "It's St John Road, St Patrick Road, St Andrew Road, and this is not The Lane it's Tee Lane because this was the tee-off of the golf course."

On return from Canada, I became Deputy Director General of the

Department of Foreign Affairs and could afford the bond repayments on the R250.000 I paid. Brenda, my then wife, was very pleased to be walkably close to Roedean School where she enrolled her daughter, Lauren. She was much embarrassed by the second-hand, powder blue, two-door, long, low Lincoln Continental with sloppy suspension, I had bought in Canada and preferred to deliver Lauren to school in the Merc.

The drawing below by Jim Weinbren is one of my last Joburg house. Judd's family now consisted of four daughters, Jilly, Penny and Robyn at Kingsmead and Jossie at St John's sister school, St Mary's in Waverley. He was still a Joburg man, exported as he was to Sandhurst as the chic spread northwards. Wayne, remarried to a Dutch girl, Dimph, had moved southwards to Walkerville, near where we had visited the Lennings. His two elder children, Brendan and Sarah, lived with their mother and he and Dimph produced two more daughters, Chantelle and Yvette. With St John and Bridie at the University of Cape Town, there were 16 people with the surname Babb in Joburg. As the daughters married and Wayne and I moved to Spain, Holland and Cape Town, after Judd's suicide, only one remained, Sarah, and she and her mother moved to Cape Town and the Babb name left the Joburg telephone directory.

Jim Weinbren's pen and ink drawing of 4 St Andrew Rd, Houghton

The Houghton house was where Edward (called Ewardie) and Katie (called Katie Puss) had their first years together. I built a treehouse in one of the large trees and a stone and cement platform next to the pool and painted the dining room a deep maroon. Living on the property were Marylynne and Andrew Hayward. She looked after the children and Andrew worked as a high-end chef at the Carlton Hotel. I had appointed the couple as chef in Ottawa and they have followed the vicissitudes of the family and of Edward and Katie through my session as member of Parliament, my posting to Rome and ever since have been an extension of our family grouping. He is a mad chef, an insane motorbike rider and a prankster, always alert to the humorous possibilities of any situation. In conversation I once mentioned that the noble families in Venice often set their table with cutlery, glassware and linen of different types to show off the wealth of their extensive and expensive houseware. The next time we sat down to dinner together, Andrew set the table with assorted silver, plastic and stainless-steel accoutrements of the weirdest kind "to show the wealth of things we had hidden in our cupboards". Both Katie and Edward took the Haywards on as alternative parents. He now lies in a coma from which he may never recover in the south of France after being knocked off his motorbike by an army truck.

The cousins Babb

The house served for receiving the heads of African diplomatic missions and garden receptions for the Africa division's foreign delegations' visits, for farewell dinners – a sort of refuge from the Pretoria claustrophobia where I could receive the mercenary, Bob Denard, and the Comorian leadership without a fuss, the demented Gaëtan Duval, former Prime Minister of Mauritius and one of his many mistresses – Brigitte Bardot was in love with this feckless man. He arrived at Jan Smuts airport once with his hands in bandages. "Did you get caught with your hands in the till?" I asked – "*Non, mes chiens m'ont mordu.*" When I stood for Parliament, it could receive donors and supporters in an atmosphere of amity and friendship conducive to writing cheques.

* * *

Each house has its own charm, its own character, its own ghosts and its own demons. My Joburg trio each raise one overwhelming moment for me. The Parktown North house we occupied after my return from Paris has one moment in which the world stood still, all sound became mute and blood drained from my head. I sat on the bath in which Ann lay and her twelve words stabbed my heart like a rapier. I confronted her with the affairs she had had in Paris and the one that lasted the longest – why? These were the twelve words: "He had a beard and looks that I liked." Would she do it again: "I don't know." They still buzz in my conscience. Twelve words to flatten all

Edward and Katie and Winston in the mud, Houghton

investment in her. To make me desperate and leave. To make my eldest son change his name.

In the Kensington house, the demon was loneliness. I frenetically worked on our Africa contacts, occupied from early morning to late night. Visiting African countries and supervising aid projects. There was one moment that epitomised that aloneness – lying in my enamelled brass-footed bath (again), my transistor played *She's Got Bette Davis' eyes* and a tear ran down my cheek at the twanging electric guitar and the melancholy tune.

The phantom's cave that released the demons lay in Houghton. That is where I lived when Bridie died. Bridie died. It was the most desolate, bleak time of my life. Expecting her for Christmas and knowing she would never again sit with a silly hat on her head. The photographs of that Christmas lunch in 1987 have an eerie emptiness that makes me ill when I look at them. The pictures fell off the wall in my bedroom and at office. A scream vibrated constantly through my body and my unseeing eyes retreated into my head. I could not have felt more distant from the world than at that time and the lack of warmth of our marriage, comfort was hard to come by. I kept on saying to myself, rather it had been me. I'd swap with her now. St John did his utmost and came almost every day of the University vac and we wandered through the garden, but what was there to say? I was bitter at the world and at God. It was the innocence of Edward and Katie that saved it and stopped my doing something rash. My character changed then. An exuberance was extinguished: let everything be against me, I don't care. I'll take it as it comes. I put a bubble plastic cover over myself and isolated myself so that the wounds would not fester. Distance was a protection for myself and my wounds. I adopted a *weltanschauung* of disconnection. I sought out people who were congenial to me and with whom I did not have to watch every word for fear of causing offence. St John joined me to go and fetch her body in Beaufort West. John Ainscough and John Sinton, the Anglo-Vaal pilots, flew us in the Hawker-Siddeley to the gravel runway and a passing farmer took all four of us to the town centre. St John and I walked to the police station and after filling in the forms, a constable took us to the cold-room and slid out the trolley on which Bridget lay. I leant over to kiss her forehead and shamefully, shamefully, recoiled at the icy skin.

St Martin's-in-the-Veld overflowed at her funeral. I sat next to Ann. I wept throughout and only remember the priest saying she would never get the four-poster bed she coveted or go on the tour of America. Her death destroyed Ann. Ann's own death by hypothermia (cold) I can only ascribe to the wretchedness that lingered with her. Even Pik and Helena Botha came to the church. I could not stand greeting the mourners and repaired to the hall where Bridie's portrait by René Marin hung. She looks inquisitively at the viewer and kneels next to a wooden macaw since René Marin asked her to pose with something quirky or dear to her.

At her cremation in the Braamfontein crematorium on Showground Road, only St John, Heidi, Ann and I attended and watched the coffin part the plastic curtain flaps into the humming maw of the oven presided over by a black clad AVBOB undertaker. By this time, I had run out of tears and my swollen eyes just bulged more.

Bridie was born in 1968 so she would be 54 now. Again: whatiffery? She was endowed with calm, humorous self-possession. Her friend, Heidi, in her class at UCT, related how a lecturer in biology had got to the sensitive subject of human reproduction in a first-year class of 250 young students. As

Bridie in her matric ball dress

he came to the end of the class, Bridie stood up and said deadpan: "I learnt early in life that the stork brought babies." Mayhem, chaos, unruliness. "No, they are found in cabbage patches." "Fairies drop them by parachute." The class dispersed in merriment. She was wont to enter a crowded elevator and say, in a loud whisper: "Then he put his hand on my boobs, and his mother saw him and shouted ..." and other inventions which had all the forward-facing elevator-riders, leaning their ears in her direction. She had a little ditty she recounted straight-faced:

"Thethil wath a caterpillar. Thethil wath MY *friend.*

The latht time I thaw Thethil, he was **this big.**

I thaid,'Thethil, what have *you done?"*

"I ate my auntth and uncleth."

Thethil wath a caterpillar. Thethil wath MY *friend.*

The latht time I thaw Thethil, he was THIS BIG!

I thaid, 'Thethil what have you done?'

"I ate my couthins and my neitheth and nephewth."

Thethil wath a caterpillar. Thethil was MY *friend.*

The latht time I thaw Thethil he was this big.

I thaid, "Thethil, what **have** *you done?*

"I've been thick."

* * *

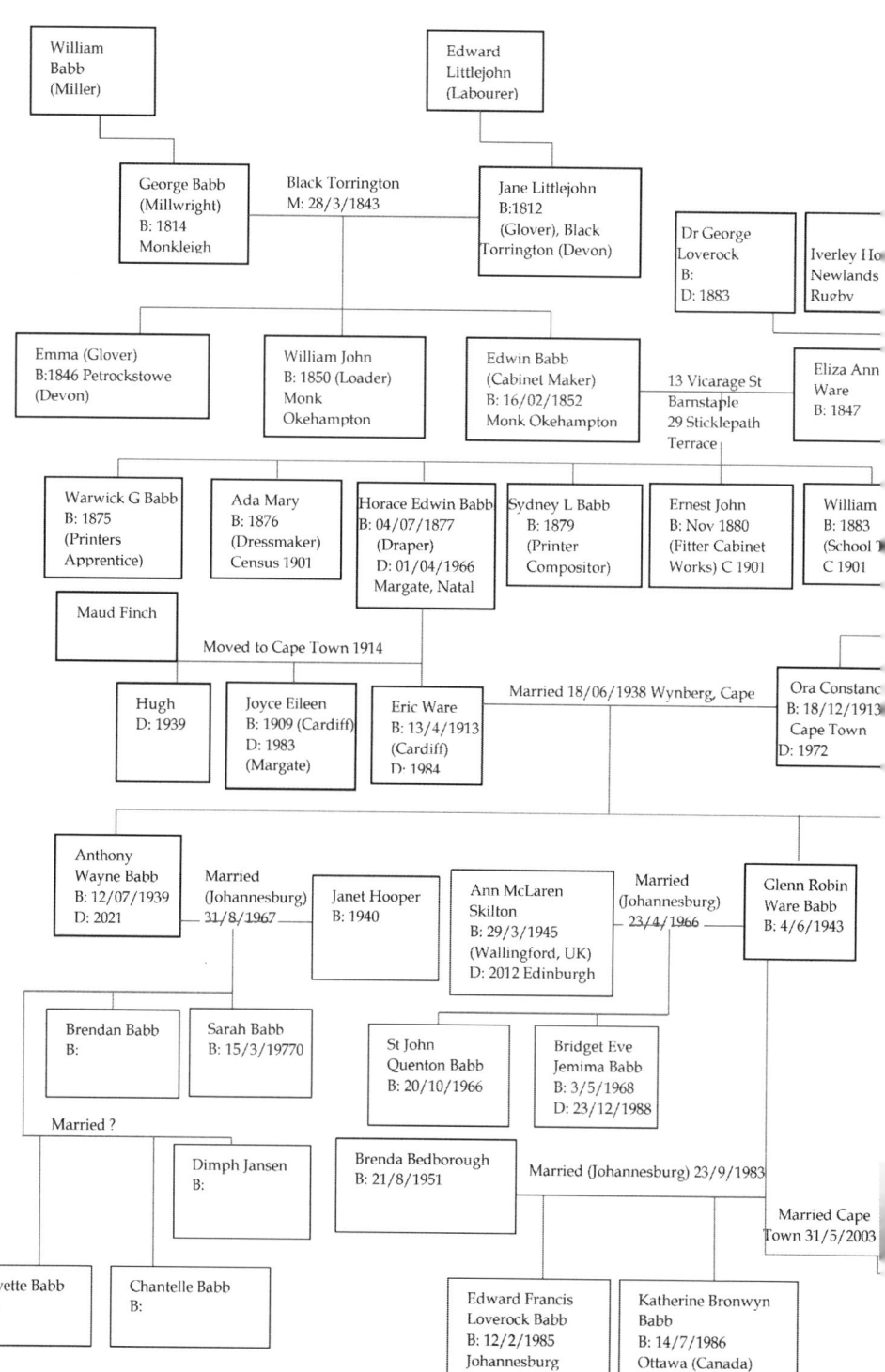
Family Tree Ora and Eric Babb

Family Tree Ora and Eric Babb

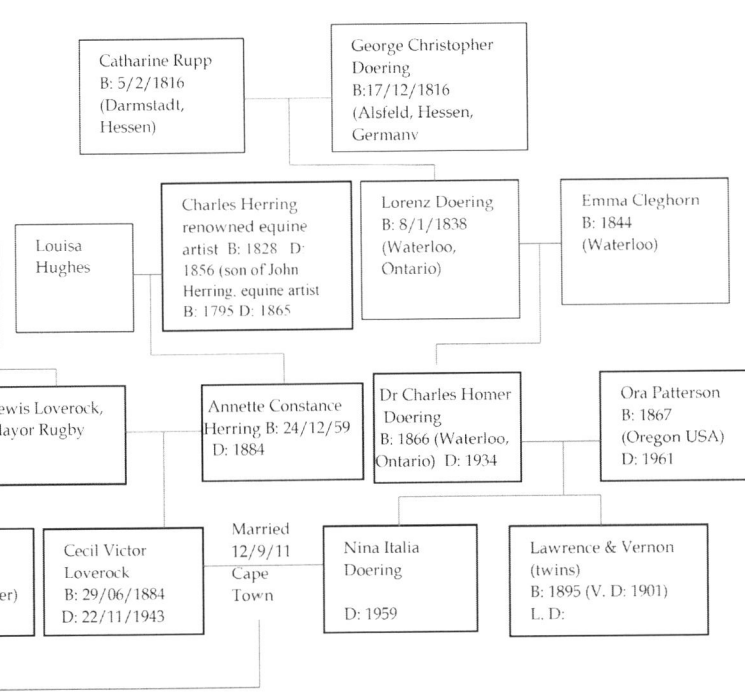

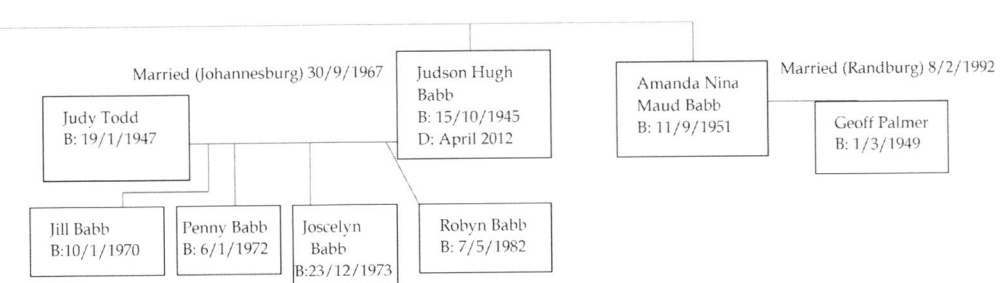

Tracey Dibb
B: 10/9/1965

Beatrix Belinda Babb
B: 14/2/2008

St John hid his deep mourning for Bridie and within three months left South Africa. He wrote me the most heart-rending letter once he had finished his chemistry degree at UCT. He was angry with our divorce, with my remarrying, with Bridie's death and with the disorder in South Africa. He was deeply hurt, and you could tell from the letter he wrote on leaving:

> "Dear Dad, I'm leaving for the United States in two days' time. I was going to send you a long and involved letter detailing my motivations for leaving and my dissatisfaction with the state – but the letter would probably only have hurt you and you would have misunderstood me. Goodbye St John."

But what a romantic life he has led. I am so jealous. He crewed in a yacht to the Caribbean and on his way back he became systems engineer at FISONS, the fertiliser company. He earned enough to buy a flat in Edinburgh where he entered Edinburgh University to study Celtic Languages, played cricket for the staff and travelled around Europe. He already spoke French and Italian and he later in his career learnt German, Japanese and Korean. Once he had his honours degree, he did a doctorate, after a period at Wollongong University in Australia, at Lausanne University and is now one of the 60.000 people left able to speak Scottish Gaelic for which he interviewed speakers in the Hebrides and offshore islands.

Squoshie the Scot

Back to the Grindstone

One of my best friends at Oxford, Tony Davey, was cherry-picked by IBM for his having done a classics degree in Greek and Latin. The same happened to St John who worked for the company Waterford Technologies and became an expert in equipment called a mass spectrometer that can identify liquids and solids in matter and was used to determine bacterial matter in a rock from Mars. From Sale, Manchester, he was transferred to Switzerland and lived near the frontier in France at Annemasse, where his first son, and my first grandchild, Benoît, was born after he married another doctor of engineering, Jen, in Australia. Over the years the anger has comprehensively subsided, and a loving relationship has re-grown between us. A relationship to include quips and ribbing. A relationship which remembers shared likes and adventures. A relationship which understands the nuances and the family in-jokes. Now he lives in Boston, Massachusetts, on semi-rural plot and in a nineteenth century house.

It was from the Houghton house that I launched my attempt to get into Parliament representing the evolving National Party. The Deputy Minister of Foreign Affairs, Kobus Meiring had encouraged me to put myself forward. In America, you run for election. In South Africa, you stand for election. FW de Klerk, leader of the Party, from his office, where he saw me, phoned Olaus van Zyl, member of the Transvaal Provincial Administration, and proposed me for the Randburg constituency where a Broederbonder, now member of the Democratic Party and a long-standing resident of the suburb, held the seat with a majority of over three thousand votes. It was a long shot, but de Klerk said to me, "If you don't make it, I'll look after you." A vague promise. Thijs Nel, my best friend and resident of Randburg said I was mad: "The Nats will stab you in the back – I know my Afrikaners." All around people shook their heads at this rashness when I was at the top of my career in Foreign Affairs and probably the next Director General. I have no regrets – Pik Botha and the Washington Mafia that ran the Department were leading us and South Africa down the wrong path and Pik had angrily said to his heads of mission, "If you don't aggressively put the government's policies to your receiving states, you can come back or I'll recall you," much to the bemusement of Denis Worrall, Carl von Hirschberg and me who were articulating the changes in South African internal politics towards a liberal democracy.

Randburg was a separate municipality then. Just north of Joburg, it had developed from agricultural plots, owned by Afrikaners into a bourgeois suburb where English-speakers now outnumbered the Afrikaners and made it an unlikely National Party preserve. The Party Committee consisted of some enlightened people. Apart from Olaus van Zyl, who was married to Karike Creuzenkamp, the famous Afrikaans singer, there was Pieter Coetzer, the author of a biography on Alan Hendrickse, the Coloured Labour Party leader, Mrs Howell and other rather jolly people. They were only too happy to have me in the constituency as no one else was daring enough to stand against Wynand Malan. They were also happy, because John McDonell, the owner of Canadian Overseas Airlines, a Rhodesian sanctions buster and the son of the IRA leader in the rebellion, put up R150.000 for the campaign. He wanted me on the board of his air transport company which I could not be while a civil servant.

The campaign was a happy and unusual one, with cardboard cut-outs of the candidate held by students at robot crossings, a roomful of students phoning the voters on the roll, joined by Cadets from my former Department of Foreign Affairs until the big knobs put a stop to that, lots of articles in the media and even a debate on TV between me and Wynand Malan during which I asked what the price of a loaf of bread was, since he had said his party wanted economic redistribution. His answer could not have been worse: "My wife does the shopping," thereby alienating not just the poor but the feminists as well. A rather sour cartoon appeared in *The Star* depicting me about to chew into a sandwich whose spread was struggling figures over the caption: "Yes and what about the price of apartheid." We were interviewed together for *Frontline* and Ruuda Landman of *Carte Blanche* came to our offices in Randburg which were situated in a house with a tennis court which had been sold to developers. Our posters were everywhere: "Glenn Babb works for You! Werk vir Jou!" I tramped the streets, day and night and was told by a Conservative Party member that if his candidate did not come and visit him, he would vote for me. Dogs barked at me, lonely old ladies asked me in for scones and tea. We participated in tree-planting at the local park and my Lincoln Continental Coupe de Ville was covered in stick on posters: "Glenn Babb works for You! Werk vir Jou!" House meetings at gentle supporters homes brought me closer to the voters, the dedicated ones that is, and hardly a harsh word was spoken.

That the campaign, rare in the annals of Nat history, made a stir was evidenced by the British and US embassy counsellors each asking for appointments to understand where the Nat Party was going. Some celebs came on board, TV personalities and a prominent Randburg businessman, Gert van der Linde, who all denounced poor old Wynand Malan. We stole a march with postal votes and were far ahead in the numbers. This contradicted an earlier poll which showed I would only get 40% of the vote. There were three Joburg English-speakers standing for the Nats including Craig Williamson who had been outed as the spy that had infiltrated the ANC in Switzerland, and we three were taken as a new tendency together in Nat thinking.

Not a day went past without our sending out a press communiqué which was faithfully recorded in *Beeld*, *The Citizen* and *The Star*. We held two big public meetings, one at Randburg High School, where a complaint was made that there was so little opposition that it was like a university lecture, the other at Robin Hills Junior School where, for the first time ever, a National Party candidate (me) appeared on the stage with a black man – Hassan Weheli – who endorsed me as a candidate who knew Africa and would prioritise Africans. This meeting was hijacked by Pik Botha, who saw an opportunity to justify his and de Klerk's sacking of PW Botha, and he insisted on a large TV screen to show the demise of PW. The hall was packed, and the press was all over the place. A heckler sat on a high windowsill and threw interjections during my and Pik's speeches, much to the amusement of the crowd. It was lively and exciting.

Other candidates asked me to speak at their meetings as I was now a drawcard. But Thijs Nel was right, previous candidates sold their second-hand Masonite poster boards to our treasurer at inflated prices to recoup their expenses at our cost. The campaign also attracted the attention of the socially upwardly mobile. I found myself being invited thrice by Marino Chiavelli for Sunday lunch at the Zoo Lake Restaurant where he had a weekly table for twelve which inevitably included Captain Ehlers, the private secretary of President PW Botha, other luminaries and always a stunning young nubile girl with her mother who contributed nil to the conversation but who left in Marino's Rolls Royce with him – a monetary and sexual tryst, encouraged by the mother for its material rewards. There was always a huge cake, the remains of which Marino had the restaurant box and handed to me. An observant diner reported this to the press implying that the box contained untold wealth for the candidate. Marino loved this and teased the journalists who called him: "Who knows what is in the box? The money or the box?" His donation to the cause was rather miserly, though.

Wayne and Judd watched all this bemusedly from afar, not quite sure that they could change their minds about the Nats, now that I was one.

FW at Randburg polling station

Back to the grindstone

On election day, 6 September 1989, I travelled from polling station to polling station and then went for lunch at Randburg Council offices with FW and Marike de Klerk, where the statisticians made an analysis of the numbers coming from the polling stations. De Klerk shook his head: "*Ons sal moeilik hierdie een wen.*" The analysts were right. At my constituency, FW de Klerk knew there would be a large press contingent and there was.

In the voting station, the tellers took each ballot and piled it onto the votes for each candidate. The doubtfuls were put on one side until the end of vote-counting and all the observers had to decide which way it was to be counted. I really liked the one ballot which rather than a cross contained ten little hearts in my square. The tellers agreed to that one going to me. The *tannies* doing the telling, as the piles for Wynand crept higher than mine, looked at me pityingly as I walked amongst them. The bundles were made into hundreds in elastic bands and the observers checked if they contained only ballots for one candidate. One pile was wrongly assigned to Wynand, who sat disconsolately and miserably on the dais steps watching the proceedings listlessly. He resigned from Parliament three months after being elected. When I crossed him on the road outside the old Senate Building, he said disconsolately: "Ek haat hierdie plek."

I lost by 1400 votes in a three-way contest, increasing the Nat vote but not beating Wynand. The Nats lost 31 seats in that election and I was the only candidate to increase voter numbers. The DP voters who feared so much in our constituency showed their elation. We got out of there quickly. There is great loneliness in defeat and all the help I had when it looked good for the Nats, melted like mist before the morning sun. I found myself touring the constituency in my Lincoln Continental Coupe de Ville "Glenn Babb works for You!" cutting down posters for which you are fined if still hanging five days after the event. Olaus phoned to say I could have a seat in the President's Council which I declined and said I would only accept one of the two nominated Parliamentary seats for the Transvaal and went off to Rustenburg to lick my wounds. I have never known such exhaustion, such flatness, such blackness. The veld did not even buoy me. But here I received a call from the Party headquarters – the Nat Transvaal caucus had chosen me as one of their nominated members – please come to Cape Town for the opening of Parliament on 10 October.

I learnt later how the caucus had voted on my membership. FW de Klerk had insisted that the caucus, of which he was leader, choose Jacob de Villiers whom he wanted in his cabinet, and select the other amongst the remaining three candidates: Louis Nel, a previous Deputy Minister of Foreign Affairs, Gerrit Bornmann, Pik Botha's candidate, and me, proposed by Olaus. After two rounds, I came out as winner which infuriated Pik Botha who summoned David Behr of the *Sunday Times* to make an *ad hominem* and vile attack on me. Behr duly published Pik's tirade and it was the Conservative Party's Koos van der Merwe who consoled me, saying he knew where the venom came from. Thijs Nel was right. The Nats would stab me in the back. It did end my ambition of becoming deputy minister of foreign affairs for which FW hinted I had been selected.

* * *

Unbeknownst to me, this was the cutting of my umbilical cord with Joburg. Now, Cape Town became my South African belly button. After a year, I sold the St Andrew Road house and, with the proceeds, I bought a house in Oranjezicht in Cape Town near where my great grandfather, Dr Charles Homer Doering had lived. With the spare change, I could afford a small flat for Mandy and her husband, Geoff, in Randburg near to the Rhema Church to which they both belonged and where I had been fêted during my election campaign.

The surname, Babb, which a whole tribe wore in Joburg, began to designate fewer and fewer people. Judd's daughters married and took other names, my parents were dead, I had left so the name was borne by Judd, Wayne and Dimph and Sarah.

Then that devastating thing happened. Judd committed suicide. Why? He seemed to me like the least likely candidate for this end. I was poleaxed. It was gut-wrenching. What had piled on his shoulders that forced this lively, amusing and bright man to shoot himself? As is always true, the blows had accumulated after his daughters left home. His wife of so many years was diagnosed with obsessive-compulsive personality disorder which made her break things dear to him, wedge out the diamond in her engagement ring and purposefully make mischief like using all the hot water so Judd could not shower. Developers had taken over the site next to his driving range and deprived him of water which made him close it down. He moved out of Dainfern which was the *summum nec plus ultra* home for which he had worked all his life. He was attacked in the Bryanston residence he rented by hoodlums led by his Zimbabwean maid, who pistol whipped him, blindfolded him and stripped the house of everything of value. The police did not follow up even suggesting he had made it all up for insurance fraud. The guards at the residence, to whom he turned with blood streaming from his head were obviously in on the act. His personality changed for ever after that and depression set in. He had to move to a smaller cottage with a sneering Polish landlord where he eventually put the shotgun to his head. I had pleaded with him to come and live with us in Cape Town but in all my calls to him he had cogent reasons why he could not – the girls, his friends – no persuading, even from Penny, his daughter would convince him.

But I place the reason even further back than this. The headmaster of St John's, Deane Yates played the cruellest trick on him by asking my father to take him out of school in his ante-matric year because the masters thought he would fail, and the school had to show good results. Judd never recovered from this insult – he had an IQ of 136, he was a swimming champ, he would have been drum major. The choice of school was my father's, but it was not the right milieu in which he could blossom. The talents he had in art would have been recognised in a more free-spirited place. Once we were at school, my parents abdicated all education and formation to the school so he was left to the mercies of little martinets like Jack Huggett and long shanks Crowther-Smith.

The last day I saw him in Joburg when I went to a Canadian-South African colloquium in May 2012, we ambled through Sandton City and visited all the clothing stores where he remarked on fashions, the source of the new wave of clothing imports, his pride at being the only person to manufacture Arrow shirts outside the USA in his Hong Kong factory and the fabrics now used. He was nostalgic and calm, but seemingly resigned to inactivity, not the go-ahead Judd we all knew. The driver's door on the Mercedes would not open and he talked vaguely of having it fixed. That Sunday afternoon visit convinced me he should join us in Cape Town, and Tracey, who knew and loved Judd, offered to welcome him into our Muizenberg house.

When Warren phoned to ask if I had heard from Judd and I said we had spoken five days before, I guessed this was the end. And so it was. Not the way I had expected. It was like a punch in the belly. Gilly, his eldest, arranged a commemoration in Randburg to which all his mates came – Mike Matthews, John Piguet, Dean Herrick – and at which I gave the eulogy reading Mandy's poignant memories of accompanying him round the garden dead-heading the flowers. His son-in-law, Graham Ford, evoked the disciplinarian in Judd – his demand for good manners, for all the conceits Mom had imbued in us.

His son-in-law, Graham Ford, brought out the disciplinarian in him – his demand for good manners, for all the conceits Mom had imbued in us.

At the time I stayed with Claude Charbonnel who had helped Judd with business in France. So that circle was completed. Claude had bought a five-acre estate in Lonehill and lamented the way Joburgers now were reduced to living in gated villages without lawns, tennis courts and swimming pools as they did when he first came to Joburg. His house was filled with Etruscan artefacts, Persian tiles, eighteenth century paintings and even an impressionist painting by Alfred Sisley. He met me when he had returned to France for a short while and I was serving at the Paris Embassy. Both he and Cecil Michaelis, who were bosom buddies, had the modesty of wealth and the assuredness of culture. He had made his fortune selling rails to Minister Paul Sauer, Minister of Transport, and never failed to recognise what South Africa had done for him, eventually taking three Zulu youth into his house, and schooling them all – one dying later of an overdose of drugs. His mastery of English was extraordinary and witty: he called Roelf Meyer "Rough my Hair." He wrote an autobiography entitled *Passeport Numéro Un* since he was the first Free Frenchman to sign up in London during the war and fought in Morocco and Italy with the allies. His hatred of Charles de Gaulle was vitriolic. "A jumped-up traitor," he called him. When he returned to South Africa after having renovated a seventeenth century apartment in the second arrondissement, scraping all the paint from ten rooms' elaborate oak panelling, he brought his major-domo with him who did not last three months because he had to shop with blacks.

It was at Claude's estate that I gathered the whole clan together. In the photo at the pool I count 24 siblings and parents, all Babbs and husbands and children and so most no longer bearing the name. It is heart-wrenching to see all these solid and dependable citizens, the end-product of the fruits of Mom's womb, now scattered and losing the bonds that 17 Park Street provided.

Wayne, in his inimitable and precise fashion, built a cottage at Walkerville and then began, with a squad of artisans and workman to construct a house to the liking of Dimph, but with this twist: it had to face due north, not magnetic north, but true north which he proudly announced to all who would listen. As Dimph retired, he moved out of the main house back to the cottage while he planned to leave for Europe and the delectable pensions offered to retired citizens of the European Union. Soon, his daughters, Yvette and Chantelle, followed him to Europe where they are now highfliers in banking and AIDS research.

Of my five children, only one was born in Joburg. St John was born in Wallingford near Clifton Hamden where I moored my houseboat, Bridie in Pretoria when I was working at the Union Buildings, Edward in Parktown in Johannesburg, Katie in Canada when I was serving in Ottawa and Beatrix in Cape Town, offspring of Tracey and me. St John attended St John's, Bridget, Kingsmead along with Judd's daughters and Edward, Katie and Beatrix went to school in the Cape but not at Mom's school, St Cyprians, so the Babb name migrates finally from Joburg.

Mandy at the top of the drive in her Redhill uniform

Mandy

The completion of my tale of Joburg leaves the most significant till last. The tale must comprise fortitude, humour, determination, sacrifice, responsibility and impishness. That is why I left till now the story of Mandy, because she encapsulates those qualities, qualities that suit Joburg. All of us were called Amanda ("requiring to be loved," said Mom) before we were born, and then Mandy came and filled the gap. Amanda Nina Maude, the forenames of her maternal and paternal grandmothers. Amanda Banana Mud Jimmy Mc Clurg called her – a kind of mud that we do not mind sticking.

All the children were born in a year of an odd number: 1939, 1943, 1945 and 1951. Mom and Dad in 1913. Mom was thirty-eight when Mandy was born. I remember the panic in the house when Dad took Mom with contractions starting when she was scarcely eight months pregnant. When Dad came back the next morning, he looked like I had never seen him before – wan and twitchy. He did not say it precisely, but things were precarious. Mom had had a caesarean section since Mandy was a *placenta previa* and Mandy was born at 3 lbs 6 oz. She went into an incubator. Dad spent much time at the hospital and the first Sunday, I accompanied him on a round of visits to clinics and hospitals all over Joburg to look for expressed milk from mothers who had excess while Mom was not producing enough for the little worm she had produced. It was touch and go. It was during a visit to the nursing home that Mom broke relations with Mickey Stewart, her oldest friend who suggested that Mandy be allowed to die. Mom was incandescent.

Mandy's strong will was evident from the beginning. She came home three days after Mom and was installed in the room across the corridor from Mom and Dad. This room had not changed since I first knew it. On the wall hung the same picture that had always been there. It depicted a man, his wife and three children in wintry clothes hauling a tree trunk, branches and sticks each according to the size of the person. Mandy occupied a drop-side cot. She looked tiny on the mattress. She so warmed my heart. My eight-year-old self often crept into the cot and lay cuddling the little worm. It gave me great comfort to feel her little heart beating against me.

From the start, Mandy was treated like any other member of the family. It was an organic thing. The family had never been anything but feet-on-the-ground. No-one sulked. Any misfortune must be dealt with by picking yourself up, pulling up your socks, facing the music, being independent and getting on with it. So it was with Mandy. She would never be treated as an invalid, she would be teased and tickled and joshed like everyone else. Because you see, it was early clear to my parents that Mandy could not see. She had been born with cataracts. Where had those come from? Mom had not had German measles. What she had had was a rash that went quickly away. I think she had toxoplasmosis, a parasitic disease caught from cats' faeces. It attacks the narrowest veins – I caught it when eighteen and it left a scar on the retina of my right eye, now hardly detectable. It is a strange disease and studies show that having it makes you particularly fond of cats which were numerous at 17 Park Street. It is transmitted by pregnant women through the placenta and can cause serious disabilities in the embryo and new-born.

The ophthalmologist, Dr Piet Boshoff, detected the cataracts immediately, but Mandy had to wait until she was eighteen months' old

Mandy learning to walk

before she could undergo the operation. It was a miracle for her seeing the features of everything around her. She did not get perfect vision. If you looked carefully at her pupils, you could see two transversal lines where the scalpel had opened the cataracts. She soon had glasses, thick but not like bottle bottoms. Mandy says that if the modern techniques and methods had existed then, how different her sight would have been and she would not have later become blind.

Black people in the shops looked at her and called her Mazawattee. On Mazawattee tea canisters and boxes, both granny and the little one, wore glasses like Mandy's. Everyone was fascinated by her. Our next-door neighbour, Caroline Serrurier especially came round of an evening to look at Mandy eating supper in her highchair. Caroline's mouth opened when Mandy's did and closed when the food went in. Her body was robust, and she stayed slim all her life growing almost to my mother's height of 5'5".

She quickly learnt to read. Her favourite spot was under the standard lamp behind Dad's chair in the sitting room where the amplified light made reading easier and more comfortable. Here, she lay on her stomach for hours and devoured all the children's books in the house. Physically she held her own. Ball games were out of the question, but she quickly took to swimming and I have heaps of photographs of the blonde girl sitting on the swimming pool steps with the children she met in the neighbourhood, at nursery school and then prep school – Graham Ford, Bridget McClurg and Jane Crozier. She was very good at socialising and made friends of every stripe.

Mazzawattee tea tin

I have written that Mandy was not cocooned or wrapped in cotton wool. She had to suffer the slings and arrows of outrageous fortune. And did she not! Uncomplaining. Never in her life has she been sorry for herself. She takes things as they come. She put up with all the banter and joshing that was in the Babb family DNA with good humour. Her laugh is something to see – she throws her head back and guffaws. One gadfly was Judd who teased her incessantly. Bumped her. Took things away so she could not find them. He did this in good spirit and loving her irritated reaction. She got her own back: when she got mumps she came and breathed heavily on me over and over, and I did catch the disease. She was sent to nursery school, like all her contemporaries, and then went to ordinary school, at first, Redhill, which Caroline Serrurier attended.

She then went to Kingsmead School which her nieces later attended. She was treated at school without discrimination. Although she was hopeless at hockey the school persisted and she did the sports the others did. She was not mollycoddled, but Mom took special care of her. She was gentle and attentive to Mandy. Mom sought all ways possible to find interests that could occupy and fulfil her. She arranged music lessons. She tried and wanted to play, but, like all Babbs, music would not be the chosen route, although when she had left home, she bought a piano but she still could not advance to the Stevie Wonder level. Mom arranged extra maths lessons for her because she struggled with numerical concepts. On Sundays, Judd and accompanied Dad or Mom who took her to the maths teacher, Mrs Powis, in

Mandy with Squosh and Bridie

far-off Randburg and, while Mandy sat with algebra and geometry, we tried to get our home-made kites up in the chill August west wind.

Mom hit gold with horse-riding. Mandy started riding at an equestrian centre near the Balalaika Hotel, in Illovo. From the beginning we knew that Mandy had a good seat and was fearless on the horses.

When she reached teenagehood, disaster. She developed glaucoma. Glaucoma is a malady of the eye where the liquid in the eyeball fails to drain properly from the trabecular meshwork between the cornea and the lens and so pressure builds up in the eyeball as the aqueous liquid cannot escape properly. Normally, glaucoma over a number of years begins to reduce the range of vision till it even becomes tubular. In Mandy's case, the pressure was so high that the retinas began to detach.

Very worried, Mom and Dad took Mandy to see the ophthalmologist, Percy Amoils, whom Mandy loved dearly. Like so many modest South African inventors, Percy Amoils had invented in 1965 a cryosurgery (freezing or cold) tool, the cryoprobe, using nitrous oxide to cool the probe and to reattach retinas. He was the surgeon who removed Nelson Mandela's cataract. Dad's colleagues in the clothing industry, the Koseff family and the Laher family, spontaneously contributed to the costs of the operations that followed, but when the money ran out, Amoils operated for free. In vain did he try to reattach the retinas. Hardly were they back in place at the back of the eye when they would start detaching again under the pressure. No one then (or even now) knows how properly to let the aqueous fluid flow out of the eye again. Mandy tried everything to alleviate the pressure. She consulted an Indian expert who visited South Africa and his recommendations included taking glycerine to lower pressure – it did, but not enough. It was after the third op that we came back from Oxford and Ann collapsed on the ship's deck when she saw that Mandy could not see us from the shore.

Her spirit remained indomitable. On the way to Joburg we stopped at Beaufort West where we slept on mattresses of mielie cobs which evinced giggling from Mandy and provided another tale to store away on her remarkable memory database.

Over the next three years, I did my Cadet training at the Department of Foreign Affairs ending up in Pik Botha's legal and South West Africa section, even accompanying Pik to Cape Town for the Parliamentary session and staying in a prefab at Acacia Park on the sandy Cape Flats, which before bore the more evocative name of "Sessie". I saw much less of the old girl and the old man, and especially, Mandy. Although Mom's cancer had not been diagnosed, she was in a sickly and weakened state. This is when and Mandy joined the Rhema Church, starting in a car showroom in Randburg. Mandy was welcomed by Ray MacCauley and his cool, gym-bodied wife, Lyndie. Although McCauley has been accused of promoting the religion of prosperity, he has defended himself vehemently and Mandy was adamant that he deserved his income. So did a lot of people as the church built its own 5.000-seater auditorium in Randburg, accommodating record numbers of congregants. He had been a body-builder and announced God's miracle when a son was born against all the use of steroids over years.

I do not knock the charismatic churches which, sure, have their ropey sides. If a congregant's car is stolen, another will come up with a second-hand one to gift the victim. A selfless group gathered around the weak and impaired and Mandy found comfort in a whole new set of friends. She was about to leave the comfort zone of school which had cocooned her all the time – she joined her school-leaver friends in jumping into Kingsmead's fountain, all in their school uniforms. Mom writes in her letters to me how she met these new friends, not unsympathetically, but rather puzzled by the combined earnestness of the people who were beyond her ken and her range of acquaintances. She was always suspicious of fanatics. Of Mandy's new acquaintances, she was tolerant and indulgent.

What kept Mandy sane was horse-riding. The stables at first used to hire out horses and Mandy went for riding lessons with some skittish horses, one of which would not let the farrier near her. The horse she bought and which understood her and was calm and well-behaved with her was *Valiant Cocktail*, a grey. Mandy sat on her as though she was glued to her. She trusted Cocktail completely. Then, in 1969, when Mandy was 18 and she no longer had sight, she entered the junior jumping at the Rand Show. I do not know if blind jumpers had competed elsewhere, but this was treated by the press as a miracle. The trick had been the offer by PYE, the radio manufacturers, of a radio system which entailed a hand-held transmitter to earphones in Mandy's ears. Judd was the enthusiastic ring-master. He guided Mandy over the jumps, took her through her paces in a figure of eight. The Springbok rider, Ernest Hayward helped to train her, and Mandy went to the Rand Show, and performed before an admiring crowd in the junior rounds.

Showing what a fine rider she was, she won on merit an amazing number of awards and the rosettes that went with them. Her greatest and most astonishing achievement was winning, at the Horse of Year, the prize for best rider on show, knocking Bill Johnson, the husband of Mary Oppenheimer into second place. Judd said to Mandy as she got the prize: "That man is livid. He is really angry."

Mandy also earned two Highly Commended awards at the Horse of the Year in 1969 and 1970, she won second place twice and got a third at the Riding Horse Show and two Highly Commended Awards at the Rand Show. This included jumping and she was competing against the senior riders.

Mandy with her characteristic guffaw, Ernest Hayward, Springbok jumper and Cocktail

My Joburg Family

OF MANDY BABB

She rides with the best because she has faith in her horse, faith in her guide, and above all faith in herself

MANDY Babb is an eighteen year old South African girl rider who competed in the Johannesburg Spring Show this year. There's nothing unusual in that, of course—except that Mandy is totally blind, and she can't see the jumps over which she guides her grey horse Cockles.

Mandy was born with a cataract in each eye, and was operated on when she was just ten months old. For the next fifteen years she could see—but only just, with the aid of special glasses.

Then two years ago, in spite of repeated surgery, she lost her sight completely.

She had always loved horses but when she could no longer see, her mother and father believed that her riding days were over. But Mandy is a determined sort of girl. She went back to school and used a tape recorder to take down lessons. And she insisted on getting back into the saddle. Following the shouted instructions of a friend, she managed to canter Cockles around the paddock.

Soon she was able to ride into open country, but could never go further away than hailing distance from her guide.

Then a South African international horseman, Ernest Hayward, heard of the girl's determination and began giving her special lessons.

Even with Hayward's help, though, she had little hope of competing in shows—until a philanthropic businessman, the managing director of a firm which pioneered mobile radio in South Africa, stepped in. He supplied a radio set: a receiver for Mandy, and a transmitter for Ernest Hayward which sends signals on an ultra-high frequency wavelength previously unused in the Republic and which is unaffected by local interference. Now Mandy can ride far from her guide and tackle the stiffest obstacles while he watches, warns and instructs.

This is probably the first time in the history of showjumping that a blind rider has been able to compete.●

From *Illustrated Life Rhodesia* 28 Dec 1969

Mandy Babb sits confidently on Cocktail, her eight-year-old grey, while brother Judd radios instructions.

Brave Mandy rides it by ear

MANDY BABB (19) rode poised and confident into the arena at the Rand show today to show her horse in the riding class.

But, near by, speaking quietly into a small radio transmitter was her elder brother, Judd, who was giving her instructions on how to direct her grey gelding, Valiant Cocktail.

After being shortsighted for most of her life, blonde Mandy went blind 3½ years ago. "I saw no reason to give up riding just because I had lost my sight. I had been riding for seven years," she said.

Her riding instructor, the Springbok Ernie Hayward, hit upon the idea of using radio-control so she could continue riding.

The system works well. Mandy, who carries a small radio in her pocket with an earphone, has never had a fall.

Judd has recently taken over the task of directing her during shows. We practise for hours, he said.

Have you ever tried to tell a blind person how to achieve a figure eight on horseback? Judd has achieved this feat.

Mandy, who lives with her family in Norwood, Johannesburg, does not go in for show jumping "because I was short-sighted I was never keen on it."

During the Riding Class today she completed a couple of small jumps in good style however, to show the co-ordination between horse and rider.

WED. APRIL 7, 1971

Mandy

Mandy was completely blind when she competed also in 1971, once again with Judd as the director, with an even better handset. He put her through her exercises and was thoroughly engaged with the enterprise, training with her for hours on end. He had got better with the exercise and Mandy could follow the instructions with ease.

The publications use the terms "courageous" and "brave" but for Mandy, I think, she competed for the hell of it and not to impress or to win.

As her residue sight deteriorated, Mandy was taken in for training with a guide-dog. The Guide-Dog Association of South Africa is an institution that excels in training dogs, mostly Labradors, for the blind. It has always astonished me that Labradors are such good guide-dogs because if ever I see a lost dog, panting and confused on the road, it is invariably a Labrador. That is what Ken and Arleen Lord allocated to Mandy. Ken had shortly before been named Chief Trainer at the Association. He and Mandy got on famously and remained friends until his death in 2013. The mistake he made in the allocation to Mandy was that Mandy still had peripheral vision so was less relying on the dog than on her own leftover sight. Some passing busybody saw Mandy trying to guide the dog rather than the other way round and reported this to Lord and the dog was withdrawn, much to Mandy's bitter disappointment. He should merely have retrained her to trust the dog. Psychologically this was a huge blow to Mandy. From Paris, where I was serving at the Embassy, I wrote a furious letter to Ken Lord, a copy of which I have kept and whose incandescence still surprises me. Shortly afterwards, Mandy went completely blind, and her orbs were removed because of their deterioration from the incessant operations.

The British Guide Dog Association has recently appointed Mandy to give the address and hand over the plaque to its patroness, the Duchess of Sussex, Sophie. This is her speech:

"I started going blind at 15 and was totally blind by the time I was 22. I was born with cataracts in both eyes and later had detached retinas and then on top of that teenage glaucoma.

I was trained with my first guide dog in South Africa when I was

21. She was a yellow Labrador called Elsa and she changed my life.

I have had five successive dogs, three together with the first one in South Africa, two British yellow Labradors and a golden retriever.

We came to the U.K in 1999 and I was trained with my first British dog three months later in Exeter. He was a cross Labrador Retriever called Bob, and I have had another two dogs since then, both Labrador Retriever crosses. My present dog is Harmony, the only black dog I have had, now retired.

I wouldn't be without a guide dog now. These different dogs all changed my life in their special ways. They have given me independence and the courage to go out with my head held high, able to do things on my own with no help, go shopping, visit friends, travel on trains, buses and even planes on my own.

I received wonderful training both in South Africa and here in the U.K. The training enabled me to have confidence in my dogs, become one with them, as it is said, it is a partnership, and the longer I have had each dog, the closer and more in tune with the dog I become. Guide dogs are always there to help if there is a problem, obviously nothing is plain sailing all the time. I can never thank these charities enough for enabling me to do all this on my own. And giving me a loving four-footed furry friend to be by my side."

She was fortunate now to have a reliable guide because Dad married the lobotomy momma, Ruth, whose husband, Arthur, had flown to a higher perch and who moved into the house at 62 Osborne Road, in Norwood. Dad and Mom had refurbished the house and made it comfortable. It had an unfortunate attribute – it lay in a triangle of roads one of which flanked the house straight from the pavement. Mandy always felt unsafe there because her window lay right at eye level for passers-by. They could, and did, look into her window and she never knew whether she was being watched. Even though thick burglar bars covered her window, she was never at home at home.

Mandy

Ruth, in one of her intemperate (and probably alcohol-inspired) beratings of Mandy for being late for supper: "If you can't come to the table on time, don't come at all" led to Mandy picking up her plate and repairing to her room, never to dine with Ruth again. This is where her churchy friends become useful. Soon one of her co-congregants had arranged for a lease of a bachelor flat on Harrow Road in Yeoville. She had worked for Ruth's family business, Glenton and Mitchell where Fred Glenton was kind to her, for a while but she moved over as receptionist with Standard Telephones and Cables, later taken over by Bill Venter and Altech. Within days she knew the extensions of all the people on the switchboard. Take her list of 400 employees and check: she repeated the number immediately. You could not catch her out. The guide-dog took her to the bus-stop and she went to work by bus, getting from the destination bus-stop to work with the guide-dog. She cooked on her own. I shuddered when she crept her finger over the edge of pots to judge the heat, depth and preparedness.

When the lease ended, Mandy wanted to be with others and she moved in with a group in a large flat along Louis Botha Avenue on the same bus route, but she had become used to her independence and could manage pretty well anything on her own. Even though she could not extract her huge cupboard from the flat, she left for Berea where she entertained her growing number of friends and I watched with trepidation as she hooked her forefinger over the pots' sides to test the contents. The Berea flat had a garden where her guide-dog could pee and poo but it also contained a Siamese cat that shrank under the bed whenever anybody new came in. The sickly-sweet cat pee smell permeated the place as the cat hovered out of sight.

When I came back from the ambassadorship in Ottawa and sold 7 St Andrew Road, Houghton, Mandy had married a fellow-churchgoer, Geoff Palmer who cared for and looked after her. He was a project manager with additional skills in all sorts of practical electrical, woodworking and mechanical repairs. It was ironic that Mandy now became a Palmer. At Redhill she had learnt the song:

> "Bill Palmer, the farmer, was not a clever man
> He planted a walnut and that is how it began"

The tree grows and grows and blocks off the house, so Bill sets about cutting it down sitting on the wrong side of the branch – tragedy. Geoff is an earnest and dedicated man who adapted to the vast Babb empire.

They married in the marriage chapel of the Rhema Church in Randburg attended by a *Sunday Times* photographer. As is typical of the congregation, the wedding breakfast and venue were offered by one of Mandy and Geoff's fellow-congregants. They asked me to make the wedding speech which was as hard to do as letting go a helium balloon.

Mandy had made a remark to me that was counterintuitive. It seems obvious that, of the five senses, sight is the one that guides us and we use the most. After all, Darwin said his theory would be only proved if we could demonstrate the development of the eye. It is miraculous to be able to see. Yet, Mandy said: "I'd rather be blind than deaf."

That gave me pause for thought. Mandy could converse with everyone, hear the doorbell and the phone ringing, she could immerse herself in music and listen to audio-books. The social nature of humans trumps all else and she has an enormous range of friends as a result.

I asked them to select a unit in a new complex in Randburg which I bought from part of the proceeds of the sale of the Houghton house. They moved in and Mandy embarked on new work – transcribing opinion polls from audio-recordings. She had sighted assistants, but she was the fastest transcriber of them all and she took this skill with her when she left for England with her husband, Geoff. This wise decision to move meant that she fell under the aegis of the National Health Service. They left the Randburg flat and settled in Bristol from which we were sent gifts of traditional Bristol glass. The expression "happy as a sandboy" came from there. Boys were sent out to mine the special sand from the hillsides. For this they were paid in gin which made them happy – as sandboys.

Mandy was a Palmer, Judd's girls were all married, so just Sarah, Dimph and Wayne flew the banner of Babb in the Joburg telephone book.

Mandy

Of the spread of the Ora and Eric genes, I have just this damaged photo of the uncles and nieces, husbands and extensive children. I suppose it is fitting that it is so out of focus. We were all dispersing physically and familiarly. It is also fitting that we should be braaiing next to a swimming pool. Bless Claude Charbonnel for giving us this last playing field.

The dispersing clan (water damaged photo)